A special word about this book
and the events of September 11, 2001

The book you are holding had just been printed and was waiting to go to the bindery when the horrific terrorist attacks of September 11, 2001, took place in New York City. The Interlink staff and I were faced with deciding what should and could be done with this volume, and what we could now tell you about bringing your family here.

After much discussion, many phone conversations, and numerous e-mails, we decided to issue the book as it was, along with this special insert. We felt that to try to remove immediately all mention of the World Trade Center and its surrounding area, substituting attractions, replacing photographs—indeed, pretending it had never existed—seemed offensive. The buildings were an important part of the skyline, of the New York environment for decades. Performing some sort of Orwellian eradication of all references to them seemed to us to dishonor the role they played in New York's urban fabric, and even dismissive of the heroism and courage of New Yorkers after the unprecedented disaster that befell their city.

To wait until things in the New York were "back to normal," whatever that is, would mean that no new books on New York could appear for years. But we have a solution for that. Updates on the continually evolving situation will be available on my website, which you can reach at:

http://www.interlinkbooks.com/nycforfamilies.html

I maintain a free website for each of my books—my attempt to make your trips as carefree as I possibly can. I encourage readers to visit them before traveling, but it will be especially important for you to check before going to New York, where the subway routes are changing frequently and attractions and even entire city blocks are being closed for inspection and then reopened when possible. My website also contains hotlinks to all the web pages listed in this book, and many others, so you can make your plans confident of having the best and latest information.

There is still nowhere else in the world like New York. Before I began to travel there on business and then to visit family, I was more than a little skeptical—it had to have been overhyped, I was sure. But I've spent an enormous amount of time in the city in recent years, and if anything, New York is more interesting, fun, and exciting than any of the hype I've ever heard. New York City is safe, and while some attractions are no longer available, or will be out of commission for some time to come, there is still far more for a family to do there than you will have time for, however long you stay.

And the tragedy of September 2001 has unmasked the real character of New Yorkers: Far from being arrogant and cynical know-it-alls as they are too often portrayed, they stand revealed as courageous, loving, indomitable people. A trip to New York City today is more than just a fun excursion, it is a lesson in resiliency, pride, and character. This is a place that, more than ever, you want your family to experience.

—*Larry Lain*

New York City
for Families

Also by Larry Lain

Paris for Families
London for Families
London for Lovers

New York City for Families

by Larry Lain

illustrations by Michael Lain and Beth Croghan

Interlink Books
An imprint of Interlink Publishing Group, Inc.
New York • Northampton

First published 2002 by

INTERLINK BOOKS
An imprint of Interlink Publishing Group, Inc.
99 Seventh Avenue • Brooklyn, New York 11215 and
46 Crosby Street • Northampton, Massachusetts 01060
www.interlinkbooks.com

Library of Congress Cataloging-in-Publication Data
Lain, Larry, 1947-
  New York City for families / by Larry Lain ; illustrations by Michael
Lain and Beth Croghan.
     p. cm.
  ISBN 1-56656-391-7
  1. New York (N.Y.)--Guidebooks. 2. Family recreation--New York
(State)--New York--Guidebooks. I. Title.
  F128.18 .L33 2001
  917.47'10444--dc21   2001003652

Printed and bound in Canada

To request our complete 48-page full-color catalog,
please call us toll free at **1-800-238-LINK,** visit our
website at **www.interlinkbooks.com**, or write to
Interlink Publishing
46 Crosby Street, Northampton, MA 01060
e-mail: sales@interlinkbooks.com

Contents

For the latest updates to *New York City for Families*,
check out our page on the web at:

www.interlinkbooks.com/nycforfamilies.html

Acknowledgements

When people know you're writing a book, they either become afraid to talk to you or they tell you everything they know. I'm blessed with friends and family members who aren't shy about offering their help, ideas, and experiences.

Of course no one is more help than my favorite traveling companion, my wonderful wife Barb, who listens, reacts, encourages, reads, edits, and endures. The guys we traveled with for so many years, sons Mike, Rik, and Doug, have all been tremendous help. Mike and his talented wife Beth are the illustrators, of course. Rik and his wife Elizabeth are actual New Yorkers and have been so generous with ideas and with taking us places that I should almost list them as co-authors. Doug lived in New York, too, before he and Sunnie were married and turns up throughout the book.

Even people I'm *not* related to have helped. Ginger and Ken Evers had lots of advice from their family trip and served as guinea pigs for one or two things in here. Phyllis Klym provided lots of travel stories and even entries and drawings from her son's travel journal. Doris Beiber shared family experiences. Many New York tourist and museum people were liberal with their time, but Danielle Boone of the New York Hall of Science was especially generous. And even my publisher, Michel Moushabeck, kept sending me envelopes and boxes (one of which must have weighed 100 pounds) full of material.

Thank you, my friends!

New York City Boroughs

Introduction

When I was a kid I dreamed of traveling the world—going to Italy, to the Middle East, to China, to India, to South America ... all the exotic places I could think of. So what did I do to make that dream a reality?

I became a teacher—and at the salaries teachers are paid, I was pretty much guaranteed that it would be a very long time before I'd become a world traveler. But it turns out that it's not necessary to buy a round-the-world ticket to experience the diversity of the earth's people. A ticket to New York City will do just fine.

Planet Earth contains something like 200 different countries. But if all the dreams of world peace and unity were to suddenly come true, the capital city of the planet would surely be New York.

New York is already the financial capital of the world. When the New York Stock Exchange goes *hic-* the rest of the world goes *-cup.* You'll find more multinational corporate headquarters in Manhattan than there are whiskers in a roomful of cats. So many languages are spoken on the streets of the city that visitors check their maps two or three times a day to make sure they haven't somehow wandered out of the United States at some obscure subway stop.

Even the United Nations has its headquarters here.

To visit New York City is to travel the world, experiencing the authentic cultures and cuisines of every nation: A visit is a world cruise that stops at every imaginable port on the globe—without ever leaving New York Harbor.

No school textbook your kids will ever have can give them this kind of richness.

Add to this the fabulous entertainment, the renowned museums, the eye-popping skyline vistas, and the single most incredible city park ever built.

Does this sound like the sort of experience you want your family to have?

Who could refuse!

People who avoid New York City are most often put off by the television shows they've seen depicting New York as an unsafe place filled with obnoxious people. Nothing could be further from the truth. New York has become one of America's safest urban areas, and its people (even the ones I'm not related to) are the most helpful I've found anywhere. Remind me to tell you the Brooklyn taxi story later. We all know that television bears little resemblance to reality; New York is an excellent case in point.

The Lains found family travel to be one of the most wonderful things we did together. When our kids were small and their schoolteacher parents were careful to budget every elusive dime, our trips were mostly limited to weekends in an adjoining state to visit grandparents. Eventually we were able to travel further afield, even to Europe. We wouldn't trade those experiences for anything.

If this book can encourage you to travel together to New York, one of the world's most exciting destinations, and can help you locate the memorable sights and experiences that will be dinner-table conversation for years to come (as, indeed, *our* trips continue to be whenever the Lains gather), it will have done its job.

Furthermore, it's the aim of this book not only to encourage you to consider a trip to New York City, but to show you how to do it affordably. We're frugal. (All right. Maybe we're tightwads.) And we found that the only thing better than a family holiday was a family holiday that cost us much less money than we had expected. *New York City for Families* will show you all the tricks and tips that make it possible.

Finally, this book will help you be something more than a tourist. *New York City for Families* will help you become a temporary New Yorker, with all the confidence and savvy of the native. All you'll lack is the accent.

Readers of other books in this series will recognize the approach. Part I will show you everything you need to know about how to eat, sleep, and get around in New York, and how to do it much more cheaply than most people—to Live Like a Local. Part II gives you a guided tour of the very best places and activities in the city for family fun. Part III will help you plan the trip carefully to make sure you don't leave anything out, and will help you figure very closely what this trip of a lifetime will cost.

Let's go! Our destination is the world's most vibrant and influential city, the meeting place for the world—New York City!

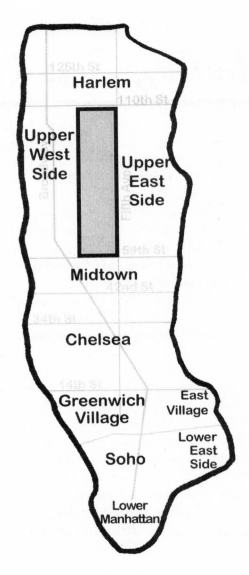

Manhattan Neighborhoods

Part I
Ready, Set, Go!

There are cities now that are bigger than New York, but you won't find one that is more diverse or more packed with things to do. That's probably why you're considering a family trip there. But you've got questions. Can we afford it? Where's the best place to stay? Is it hard to get around? What about safety? All those questions and many, many more will be answered in the first eight chapters of *New York City for Families*.

Family travel is terrific, and in the first section of this book I hope to convince you that New York will make a great destination for your family. Not only can you cope with the pace and complexity of the city, you can thrive there, becoming temporary New Yorkers yourselves. Whether you're coming from just across the river in New Jersey or from halfway round the world, this section will give you the lowdown on everything you need to know to eat, sleep, travel, and live in New York in comfort and confidence. Even if you've never been here before, you'll have a command of the day-to-day details of life in New York, and be ready to make your dream trip a reality.

Most complicated things are just a series of small details. In this section we'll handle all those details, freeing everyone in your family just to get on with the business of enjoying their time together in New York City.

1. Planning the Big Trip

Families can do so many wonderful things together, from boisterous games to quiet walks in the woods, from elaborate birthday dinners to just making popcorn, from a trip to the corner store for a candy bar to a trip—to New York! What an idea!

Just imagining a family trip to New York City will set your head spinning. How do we get there? Isn't everything terribly expensive there? Where do we stay? Won't it cost a lot of money? How hard is it to get around? Is it safe? There's so much there—how can we choose what to do? Can normal people afford a trip like that?

Relax. That's why I'm here. I *want* you to take your family to New York City, and I'll answer all those questions for you and a lot more in the next 200 or so pages. Here's why: Family travel was one of the most terrific things the Lain family did while the kids were growing up, something that brought us together and bonded us the way few other things did. If I can do something to help your family share the same kinds of wonderful experiences and create the same kinds of warm family memories, I'll be delighted.

What's more, I'll show you how to plan your trip so you can live on whatever your budget allows. The mistaken notion that I couldn't afford it kept me out of New York City for a long time. I missed a lot! Oh, if you want, I can direct you to hotels where rooms cost $2,500 a night and to restaurants where you can spend $200 per person on dinner, but I suspect those things are as much beyond your budget as they were ours.

Actually, it's a lot more fun to live economically. The visitors who stay in the fancy hotels and dine in the elegant restaurants won't enjoy their stay any more than you will at a fraction of the cost, and they will never get the real *feel* of New York City the way *you* will if you Live Like a Local. This book is your guide for doing just that.

Planning: The Second Best Part of the Trip

Only one thing can compete with the excitement of taking a trip: *Planning* the trip! Whether we're going to a place for the first time, or returning to somewhere we've enjoyed in the past, the planning stage gets us ready for what's to come. The planning process gives us a chance to talk about the kinds of things that are possible to see and do at our destination, about things we've enjoyed doing in other cities that might have equivalents here, about new sights and experiences that are possible only in the city we're preparing to visit. And this is just as true now that my wife Barb and I mostly travel alone as it was before our kids were grown and we were planning family trips.

Planning sets the stage. It gets people excited by the possibilities and gives everyone something to look forward to. Planning gets people familiar with the basics of a destination long before they get there so they get oriented more quickly when they actually arrive and know what to expect from the city.

To get the absolute most out of a family trip, though, there is only one firm rule to follow: *Everybody helps...* because this trip is for *everybody*. That's really what this book is all about. Part One lays out the strategies you'll need to thrive in New York: where to stay, how to get around, how to make the very most of your money, how to live as comfortably and economically as a genuine New Yorker. In Part Two you will visit the very best of what the city has to offer for families, including lots of places visitors don't ever find. Part Three puts it all together with a list of attractions your family can use to make decisions, a set of realistic itineraries, and some forms to make your budgeting easy.

Everyone in the family who's able should read the book—If you want to buy each person his or her own copy I won't object!—and then talk about what you've read. Dinnertime is a great opportunity for that. Reading and talking about a big trip will get everybody excited, will help crystallize plans, and will make everyone feel like they have a real stake in the trip's success, because they're not just along for the ride—they've helped with the planning.

Can We Really Afford This?

That question keeps more people at home than any other single thing. And notice I said that it's the *question* that keeps people home—not the *answer*! The question itself is often so intimidating that people just give up right away.

Don't! I'm going to show you some ways to economize on money without economizing on fun. As our kids began to get bigger, we realized that, if we wanted to show our kids something of the world outside their own neighborhood, we couldn't afford *not* to find a way to travel. And there's very little money we consider having been better spent. This book will show you many, many ways to economize so you can take this trip of a lifetime together.

The first step is to get organized, to figure out what costs you can control and what you can't. Let's begin with the category in which you will probably have the least flexibility: travel.

Planning the Big Trip

Getting to New York City

Unless you're coming from the eastern one-third of the United States or from southeastern Canada, you have very few options for getting to New York City: You're going to have to fly. Starting a holiday with a drive of 1,000 miles (1,600km) isn't a very relaxing beginning for a vacation. So you're stuck paying whatever the airlines decide you have to pay, and this will probably be the single most expensive and least controllable part of your trip.

If you *are* coming from somewhere closer, however, you have more choices. But either way, whether you're starting from Europe, or the Pacific, or Pennsylvania, Chapter 3 will lay out your choices and show you how to make the most of your money, whether that means minimizing your airfare if you have to fly, or finding ways to cut down on the cost of parking if you drive.

Living in New York City

Here are costs that are easier to control. You have an impressive range of choices about where and how to live in the city, and a correspondingly unlimited range of ways to save money. To be perfectly honest, we've always had tremendous fun looking for ways to cut our costs; it makes us feel like we're real people living real lives, not just tourists living fantasy lives. Learning to Live Like a Local is at the heart of our travel philosophy.

The best way for us to assess and compare costs for family travel, we've found, is to calculate expenses on a *per-person, per-day* (PP/PD) basis. The day-to-day cost and how-to of living in New York will be addressed in detail in the chapters that follow, but let's just take a quick look now.

Accommodations: If you want to spend lots of money, there are three unrivaled places to do it: Buy a private Caribbean island, corner the international diamond market, and get a hotel room in New York City for a week. An acquaintance told me, as I was working on this chapter, about his impending trip to the city and how lucky he felt to be able to find a hotel room at just $350 per night. Yikes! You don't have to pay that kind of money!

Chapter 2 will show you how to find accommodations for your family with more room and more comfort for less than half that amount. You might have to make your own bed in the morning, but for goodness sake—you do that at home anyway! How much would you be willing to pay someone to come in and make your bed at home every day?

Our favorite accommodation solution is to rent an apartment for a week or two. It sounds strange to someone who's never done it, but consider: Even a small apartment has more room than a large hotel room, there's always a kitchen where you can prepare some of your own meals—a terrific money saver—and a week's rental of an apartment is always much less than paying for seven nights in a comparable hotel room. Simple! Best of all, you're living like a local, blending in with the pace and pattern of life in the city in a way that's impossible for hotel dwellers.

If you *want* a hotel room, on the other hand, Chapter 2 can also help you find what you need for much less than my (apparently) wealthy acquaintance.

So how much must you pay? For a family of four, $35 per person/per night is perfectly possible. A couple of hours of work can cut a substantial amount off that. It might be a bit more PP/PN for two or three people, but even less for five (as was our case) or more.

Food: This is a deceptive category. You're not spending as much for food as you think because you'd be eating even if you stayed home! So even when you tally your food bill after your holiday, deduct what you *would have spent* at home to get a more realistic picture of your costs.

Staying in an apartment not only lowers your cost of accommodations dramatically, it means you can spend *much* less for food. When you stay in a hotel, every meal must be eaten in a restaurant. That gets expensive fast! The cost of one dinner in a moderately priced restaurant can buy enough food at the local grocery store to provide most of your groceries for a week.

If you have breakfast in your apartment each morning, you can fix the same things you usually do at home—cereal and toast, eggs and bacon, whatever you're used to. The familiar food and routine will make life easier for the kids... and consequently for Mom and Dad.

Have lunch while you're out and about, and fix a simple dinner back at the apartment most nights. Restaurant lunches are much cheaper than dinners. At dinnertime in your apartment, everyone gets a chance to take off their shoes and relax after a busy day of sightseeing. Restaurants normally discourage shoeless customers.

So how much? With groceries for two meals a day and lunch on the run, plus a special evening or two out and assorted snacks, $15 PP/PD is quite possible, perhaps a little more or less, depending on the ages and appetites of the kids. (This is variable, of course. There was a point at which our three sons were all growing, hungry teenagers. The memory still gives me chills.)

Attractions and Sightseeing: Every day will be different. Some days you'll spend nothing at all in this category, frolicking in Central Park, gawking your way down Fifth Avenue, splashing in the ocean at Rockaway Park Beach. But the next day you can spend a bundle on rides at Coney Island or hitting a couple of museums followed by tickets to a baseball game. What's reasonable? Well, watch for cut-priced tickets. Most museums have student or children's rates, and many other attractions do, too. Take advantage of all the other discounts you can think of, too, like those sometimes offered to auto club members or reciprocal memberships between museums in New York and museums you may belong to at home. *Always* ask what discounts are available, and take advantage of reduced or free admission on certain days of the week or after a certain hour. You ought to be able to see everything you came for by averaging less than $10 PP/PD.

Shopping: I don't have the slightest idea. In a couple of hours along Fifth Avenue you can spend more money than the gross national product of a developing nation without even breathing hard. Or you can spend a week in the city and buy nothing but the daily paper. Every family is different. If it's made, it's for sale in New York City. But the best souvenirs usually aren't the big-ticket items; they are the smaller items that evoke the memory of a day or an experience. Lain souvenirs are more likely to be a CD of the musical we saw, a coffee mug with the name of the diner where we stopped to escape from a sudden downpour, a 50-year-old city guidebook from a second-hand bookshop in Greenwich Village. Each of those will cost just a few dollars, and each will bring a memory and a smile each time it's used. Along with our photographs and travel journals, that's really all we ever bring home.

Let kids carry their own money, if they're old enough, and choose their own souvenirs. You might think a little plastic Empire State Building is a real waste of money, but it might very well sit on the 8-year-old's bookshelf until she goes away to college. Memories are funny things. You *want* the kids to think about this trip often, and to smile when they do. That's what those knick-knacks do. Just $5 to $10 PP/PD should be plenty, and provide the occasional afternoon ice cream cone as well.

Local Transportation: Some friends went to New York City a few years ago and budgeted what I thought was a hugely unrealistic amount in this category. Turned out they were planning to take taxis everywhere so they wouldn't get lost… or mugged in the subway. It took me a little while to convince them that the subways were perfectly safe and that they couldn't get lost so badly that they'd never find their way home again. I hope you're easier to persuade. Honestly, New York isn't at all like what you see in all the police movies and television shows. I've spent a lot of time in the city and haven't yet seen a shooting or a car chase.

Actually the subway is the best bargain in New York. It covers everywhere, it's fast, it's inexpensive, and it's air-conditioned in the summer. What a deal! You can ride anywhere in the city for the same fare ($1.50 as this went to press; check my web page for updates) and discounts are available. In fact, the first thing I do when I get into the city is to buy a one-week pass. Even if I make just two round-trip journeys per day, it more than pays for itself in less than three days. So $3 is plenty in this category. Chapter 6 teaches you all the tips and tricks of getting around.

Let's look at the bottom line, then. Here's what New York ought to cost you on a PP/PD basis on a perfectly reasonable budget:

Accommodation	$25 to $50
Food	$12 to $20
Attractions	$5 to $10
Shopping	$5 to $10
Getting Around	$3 to $4
The Bottom Line:	**$50 to $94 PP/PD**

Remember that this covers *everything* but the cost of getting there—food, lodging, sightseeing, the works! And, frankly, it's possible to spend even less without suffering a bit or living in an apartment above an all-night massage parlor. It's just a matter of Living Like a Local instead of like a tourist.

I'm Convinced. When Do We Leave?

One nice thing about New York City is that it's always there when you want it. If you can travel between November and

March (except at Christmas and the Thanksgiving holiday in late November) you can probably save a significant amount of money on airfare. Hotel and apartment prices may be a little lower then as well, but not always, because New York is a major convention city. So aside from the airfare issue, there's not as much difference between summer prices and winter prices as there is in some other places.

Go as soon as it's convenient.

I really mean that. The kids will get so much out of this trip, and it will be so much fun for the family, that *whenever* you go, you'll wish you had done it sooner. In the other books in this series I've suggested that children younger than ten might get less from a trip like this than older kids, and that's probably true of New York, too. But there are so many things for young children to do in New York, that they'll enjoy it at almost any age. I'm not sure that when our three boys were three, six, and seven would have been the best time, but by the time they were six, nine, and ten they were ready for almost anything, and that's when we began traveling.

Don't go rushing off without careful planning

—10—

How long to stay depends on how far you're coming from (and yes, of course, on how much money you have). You want to have time to make the trip worthwhile, so consider a formula of one day for every two hours of travel time. Someone driving from Pennsylvania might get by with three days in the city, for instance, but a visitor who had flown twelve hours from Tokyo would probably find so little time to be merely frustrating; a stay of at least a week would be more like it.

So go next summer or during a break from school. New York has a different face to show during every season and there is no bad time to go. The only mistake you can make is to put it off too long.

Recommendations

✔ Encourage *every* member of the family to read this book and to take an active part in the planning

✔ Calculate your costs except travel on a Per Person/Per Day basis to get the most realistic picture of expenses.

✔ Stay long enough to unwind and become a temporary New Yorker.

2. Finding Your New (York) Home

N ew York might be the city that never sleeps… but you'll have to. Finding the place to do it—Ah! That's the challenge. New York City hotels can be breathtakingly expensive. Hotels can easily charge more *by the night* than we pay *per month* for our home mortgage… and I'm not exaggerating even a tiny bit about that. Even the most chauvinistic New Yorkers will admit that housing costs are unreasonable, unfair, unrealistic—and unavoidable.

You *can* afford to take your family to New York, though, and I promise you won't have to sleep in a cardboard box in Central Park. I have a strategy or two that can save you plenty, and make your trip more fun and relaxing besides.

What Are Your Choices?

When I began outlining this book, my biggest worry was leading you to affordable accommodations. Depending on where you're coming from and how you're getting to New York, this will be either your largest or second-largest expense, and can be a deal-maker or deal-breaker for planning a big-city holiday.

Finding Your New (York) Home

Generally speaking, major American cities have fewer lodging choices than European cities, and while in most places in the United States it's easy for drivers to find inexpensive motel rooms, it is much harder to find cheap center-city hotels, short-let apartments, or B & B's.

The situation is far from hopeless, however, even in New York. A little creativity and a bit of time on the telephone or the internet can produce amazing savings on your lodging costs and get you a place to stay that's almost as comfortable as home. Let's look at what your options are. The first two are the most common ideas people have, but keep reading—the real money savers come after that.

Hotels

This is the choice most people make. Hotels are convenient. Hotels are easy to find. Hotels are... terribly expensive.

The worst thing about hotels is that you have to pay for a lot you don't need. I like to look at glittering marble lobbies hung with rich fabrics and crystal chandeliers. But I can walk through the Waldorf Astoria for free and do that. If I want 24-hour room service, I can pay a cadre of people perfectly good money to stand around in case I get hungry at 3 A.M.—or I can walk to the fridge myself and fix a sandwich for about one-twentieth what my room-service sandwich would cost. Instead of having a fully equipped fitness center at my disposal, I can take a walk.

Who do you think pays for the marble lobbies, all-night waiters, and rowing machines in fancy hotels? *You* do... every time you stay in one. Do you get your money's worth out of them? That's not what most family holidays are all about.

Even moderately priced hotels in Manhattan are more expensive than those you'd find almost anywhere else. But looking in the boroughs *outside* Manhattan is merely frustrating. Brooklyn, by itself, would be one of the largest cities in the country, but it has just a handful of hotels, most of them remote

Bringing Down the House

How can you be sure you're getting the best price for accommodations in New York? It's not easy, because housing costs are as variable as airfares. Hotel managers agree (privately, usually) that there's just one standard rule: Never pay rack rate. Rack rate is a hotel's "official" rate—but it's almost always negotiable. This applies to apartments as well.

It's important to speak to the manager directly, however. Reservations clerks, sales agents, and toll-free line operators are seldom authorized to sell anything but the published rates or standard discounts. So telephone during the normal business day when the boss is available. It helps to be able to ask for him or her by name. The operator who answers your call can tell you that.

You'll get more help if you tell managers right away that you're trying to get the lowest possible rate so you can afford to take this special family vacation. Get them on your side: They may be parents themselves.

Flexibility is important. If you are not tied to specific dates but can come when hotel or apartment bookings are slow, you'll always be rewarded with a lower rate. If you can provide your own bed linens for a rollaway, or bring a sleeping bag so one of the kids can camp out on the floor instead of use an extra bed, you might not be charged for an extra person. Agreeing to forego fresh sheets and towels every day can bring the price down in some places, and that shouldn't be a hardship unless you normally wash sheets and towels every day at home.

from where you want to be. Queens is worse, except near the airports, which in any case would involve time-consuming trips in to most attractions.

It is possible to find relatively good hotel prices, but it takes equal parts of persistence and good luck. The appendix to this book, *Websites for Planning Your Trip*, provides several hotel listings sites. Those sites will take you to links that allow you to comparison shop right online, checking prices, locations—and amenities, in case 3 A.M. sandwiches really *are* important to you.

The New York Convention & Visitors Bureau also publishes a guidebook, its *Official NYC Guide*, that lists about 140 hotels and general price ranges. It's less useful than similar guides published for

London or Paris (which list *hundreds* of hotels), but also includes information on museums, shopping, and other attractions. You can get a copy by phoning the NYCVB at +1 212-397-8222. The fax number is +1 212-245-5943. Write to them at

New York Convention
& Visitors Bureau
810 Seventh Avenue
New York, NY 10019

Before you book a

Sometimes just joining a hotel chain's free incentive program can pay dividends. One chain upgraded me from a regular room to a suite just because I was a member. Another hotel in the same chain gave me a rate that was 25 percent less than the discount rate I'd agreed to just because I was a member.

You might pay different rates for different days; weekend days are usually charged at a lower rate—be sure to request that after you've made your best deal. Always ask about other packages and incentives that might be in effect for the dates you want, or for nearby dates. Hotels will often extend special offers to customers who are polite, friendly, and flexible.

There really seems to be only one rule: Don't pay rack rate.

hotel, though, be sure to read the sidebar in this chapter, *Bringing Down the House*, for tips on getting the best available rate.

Staying outside the City

My first thought for this chapter was to do what Barb and I have occasionally done when traveling alone: Look for less expensive lodgings in the suburbs and take public transportation into the city each day. Hotel and motel prices are much lower out of the city.

This might not be the best choice for a family, though. To save a significant amount of money, you might have to spend 30 to 60 minutes on the train to get into Manhattan, buying round-trip tickets at $6 to $10 each. That's not bad for one or two people but it raises the cost for a family of five, for example, by quite a bit. It also makes it more difficult to go "home" to relax for awhile in the late afternoon before heading out for an evening activity.

Considering the extra commuting time involved before you can even begin your sightseeing day and the additional expense of coming into the city, this probably is not a good option for a family.

Now—before you go any further—stop here and read the sidebar *Cooking Up a Great Holiday*. When you've finished, come back and read about the next two options.

Hotels with Kitchenettes

This was an option we discovered on a trip to Washington, D.C. when our kids were small. Many low- and mid-priced hotels have large rooms or suites that include a small kitchen. What a find! Instead of eating out every night we could go back to our suite (which cost at that time about $10 per night more than a regular room and had twice as much space), spread out, and relax. After a simple meal we could decide how to spend the evening.

We discovered later that rooms like that aren't uncommon, and a few hotels positively promote them. The listings in the appendix under *Hotels and Suites with Kitchenettes* should help you find this middle ground between hotel and apartment living. The listings in the NYCVB booklet *Official NYC Guide* also includes several hotels with kitchenettes. Rooms might cost a little

Hotel room service is not your best dining option.

more than standard hotel rooms, but they often don't. The added space and the savings on restaurant meals are more than worth a small additional charge. Besides, you might even find a place that provides a light breakfast in the mornings, or other hotel amenities like a pool.

Other medium-priced hotels may also have options like this. Be sure to ask. Pay attention, though. There are many all-suite hotels, usually fairly expensive, but most don't have cooking facilities.

Apartment Living

This is some of the best advice in the Family Travel series. (I really should put it at the end of the books to make sure you read the whole thing….) Rent an apartment.

Cooking Up a Great Holiday

Isn't a vacation supposed to be a time to get away from regular life? What kind of holiday is it if you cook some of your meals instead of eating in restaurants all the time?

Inexpensive. Economical. Cost-effective.

If you want to make a vacation to an expensive place like New York affordable, doing some of your own cooking is an ideal way to help cut your costs. Consider that you can buy a box of pasta, a head of lettuce, a loaf of bread, and a can of spaghetti sauce for less than $10. Then fix a quick and easy supper that will fill up a family of five just as effectively as the same plate of noodles at a Midtown restaurant where the bill for all of you will come to $75.

The single greatest money-saving strategy in this book is to stay in accommodations where you can prepare some of your own meals. If you have breakfast in your apartment or hotel every morning, and are able to fix most of your dinners there as well, the amount of money you save can be substantial.

We'll go over this ground again when we talk about food in Chapter 5, but if you're budgeting for your accommodations now, keep in mind that this is a good way to save your family $50 to $100 or more per day on this trip.

This seems a bizarre suggestion to someone who has never done it, but the Lains—and thousands of other people—have found that the advantage in both comfort and cost makes this the very best way to travel. Short-stay apartments are not as numerous or as easy to find in the United States as they are in Europe, but New York City does have several reliable agencies that specialize in just this sort of thing, if you know where to look.

One place you won't get much help from is the NYCVB booklet. It lists only a couple of apartments, and they require minimum stays of a month and shocking amounts of money. The companies listed in the *Apartment Services* section of the appendix, however, are all well-established companies that offer a wide variety of apartments for visits of a few days or longer. Among them, they handle hundreds of flats, mostly serving as a booking agency for private owners, in all parts of the city, but with most properties in Manhattan.

Apartments have many wonderful advantages over hotels. Even a small apartment will be larger than the most expensive single hotel room in town. Studio apartments usually have enough room for separate sitting, eating, and sleeping areas, as well as a full bathroom; they can accommodate three people easily. One and two-bedroom apartments give everyone a chance for more privacy, something that becomes more desirable as the vacation grows longer, and provide more room than a suite at the Plaza. An apartment is more like home, with comfortable furniture, often a stereo or CD player, and a refrigerator to keep snacks and cold drinks. We've already established the wonderful savings of being able to prepare some of your own meals (and I warn you now that we'll return to this point repeatedly).

What about the price? It will vary by the size and location of the apartment, of course. But it's certainly possible to find a roomy apartment at less than $1,000 a week. If that seems like a lot— look at the price of ordinary hotel rooms. A price like $1,000 a week is about $35 per person/per night for a family of four. And even less expensive places are available to the savvy visitor.

Many of the suggestions for getting the best price in the sidebar *Bringing Down the House* apply to apartment rentals as well as to hotels.

Booking Your New York Home

Discuss what type of accommodations will best suit your family's needs and preferences. Then you're ready to browse through the listings in the NYCVB booklet and the websites in the back of this book. If you have a travel agent who has spent a lot of time in New York, you can usually get a good list of lower-priced hotels there, too. Travel agents are less likely to know about apartment rentals, but it never hurts to ask.

Unless there is a particular part of the city you *really* want to stay in, I'd encourage you to be flexible about that. It's fun to stay in a hotel overlooking Times Square, but you pay dearly for the privilege. Accommodations in Soho might cost only half as much, and be less than a fifteen minute subway ride from Times Square. An apartment in Brooklyn will cost less than one in Manhattan, but transportation is easy and you'll be living more like a real New Yorker.

Even if you do most of your research on the internet, however, I'd encourage you *not* to book that way unless you find a real deal. You're usually better off using the telephone so you can talk directly to the manager, get the information you need, and bargain for the best price.

Questions to Ask

Once you've found three or four likely-looking places to stay, you're ready to get on the phone. It will cost more than booking online, especially if you're calling internationally, but only the manager will be able to give you the best price, depart from established policies, or provide the extras that will make your stay more comfortable. Reservations sales agents either at a hotel or at toll-free numbers can seldom do those things, and when you book online, of course, you're not dealing with a human at all but with a soulless computer.

Chapter 21 will provide budget worksheets and forms you can fill out for each hotel or apartment you investigate. Here are some questions you want to ask.

For a hotel:

- Where is the hotel? What's the nearest subway?
- How large is the room?
- How is the room furnished? (*Applies to larger rooms with kitchenettes: You'd like extra chairs, dining facilities, etc.*)
- What is the charge for extra people?
- Are rollaway beds available for extra people?
- If we don't use a rollaway or if we bring our own linens for it, is there a deduction?
- How far away is the nearest self-service laundry?
- How often is the room cleaned and linens changed?
- Is breakfast provided?
- What kind of security facilities does the hotel have?
- What other amenities does the hotel have?
- What kind of appliances and equipment does the kitchenette have? (*if applicable*)
- How large is the refrigerator? (*if applicable*)
- What is the best price you can give me, including all taxes?
- Is there any way to reduce it further? (*length of stay, weekend specials, etc.*)

For an apartment:

- What is the address of the apartment? What's the nearest subway?
- How large is the apartment? How many beds?
- Describe the building. When was it last remodeled?
- Describe the neighborhood. Is it residential, commercial, industrial?
- What kind of bath/toilet facilities are in the apartment?
- Does the apartment face the street? How quiet is it?
- Describe the furnishings and appliances in the apartment.
- Describe the cooking facilities in the apartment.
- Does the apartment have laundry facilities?
- Is the apartment air-conditioned in the summer?
- What kind of security facilities do the building and apartment have?

- How often is the apartment cleaned and linens changed?
- How far away is the nearest self-service laundry? Grocery store?
- How do we pick up the keys?
- What is the best price you can give me, including all taxes?
- Is there any way to reduce it further? (*length of stay, weekend specials, etc.*)

After three or four conversations like this, you can have considerable confidence that you're getting just what your family needs, and at the best price available.

This process is more time consuming that just calling a telephone number for a hotel chain. But frankly, the research is part of the fun, and you learn a lot more about your destination and about what to expect by doing it this way. You'll also end up with nicer facilities and a lower cost. And if you want, you can download a photo of the marble-and-crystal lobby of the Waldorf Astoria and tape it to your refrigerator so any time you want to gaze at it, you can... for free!

The Mariott Marquis on Times Square has the tallest hotel atrium in the world

New York Neighborhoods

You know that New York City consists of five boroughs: Manhattan, Brooklyn, Queens, the Bronx, and Staten Island. But those are only the formal divisions. Any city as large and as complex as New York has countless informal and unofficial communities, areas, and neighborhoods, and they turn up throughout this, and every other, book that deals with the city.

Unlike the boroughs, New York's neighborhoods have no official boundaries, so it's impossible to say exactly where one blends into the next. But here is a primer, at least, of Manhattan's principal areas as they're used in this book. The other boroughs have neighborhoods, too, but since few visitors find it useful to distinguish between Flushing and Astoria in Queens or Park Slope and Bensonhurst in Brooklyn, the names of neighborhoods in boroughs outside Manhattan are seldom used.

Here, then, is a look at some of the Manhattan neighborhoods we'll be visiting in New York City for Families. *You may encounter others not used here, but overly partitioning the city is more confusing than helpful for a newcomer. Principal neighborhoods are marked on the map on page xii.*

Manhattan Neighborhoods, from North to South

Harlem: *North of Central Park and 110th Street, this area has long been home to vibrant black and Hispanic communities. Neighborhoods like Morningside Heights and Spanish Harlem are found here. Harlem offers great food and entertainment, inexpensive shopping, and the occasional glimpse of a former U.S. President.*

Upper West Side: *This area between Central Park and the Hudson River from 59th to 110th streets is home to the Natural History Museum, Lincoln Center, and many elegant apartments. This is an area favored by celebrities who live in the city.*

Upper East Side: *Between Central Park and the East River from 59th to 110th. "Museum Mile" runs along Fifth Avenue here and Madison Avenue provides expensive shopping—completely in keeping with the area's upscale nature.*

Midtown: *The beating heart of New York; the theater district. Loaded with hotels, restaurants, and attractions. The area runs the width of Manhattan from Central Park down to somewhere in the mid-30s. You might hear it subdivided into the West Side, Theater District, and East Side.*

Chelsea: *Popular, and increasingly trendy, residential area on the west side, just north of Greenwich Village and south of midtown. It includes the Garment District.*

Greenwich Village and the East Village: *Known as an artsy, bohemian area running from 14th Street to Houston Street, the Village is home to New York University, Washington Square, great clubs and restaurants, interesting shopping, and accommodations that might cost less than those in Midtown.*

Soho and Tribeca: *Trendy areas full of galleries, restaurants, and apartments, Soho and Tribeca are between Houston and Chambers streets and west of Broadway. The names are acronyms for SOuth of HOuston and for TRIangle BElow CAnal.*

Lower East Side: *Once a haven for immigrants, you'll now find many popular historical and cultural attractions here. Neighborhoods include Seaport, Little Italy, Chinatown, and Civic Center.*

Lower Manhattan: *You're certain to spend time here, at the southern tip of the island. The Battery and the Financial District are down here. You'll come down here to go to the top of the World Trade Center, to visit the Statue of Liberty, or ride the Staten Island Ferry.*

Recommendations

✔ If you're staying a week or more, rent an apartment. It's more like home and can save you money.

✔ Hotel rooms with kitchenettes are ideal for short stays and often cost little or nothing more for the extra space and facilities.

✔ Much of your initial screening and comparison shopping can be done conveniently on the Web.

✔ Speak directly with hotel and apartment service managers for the best prices. Never pay rack rate.

3. Travel Made Easier

What's the worst thing about travel? Travel. If you've ever done the least amount of traveling with your family, you know exactly what I mean. *Being* somewhere together is some of the most fun you'll ever have... but *getting* there in the first place can be an altogether different story. Preparing for a family trip can seem like a cross between outfitting an Arctic expedition and being road manager for a circus, without the fun of getting to ride the elephants.

That's why this chapter is here, to lay out the travel possibilities—including one or two you might not have thought of—and to reduce the stress of getting to New York so everybody starts out this great trip as friends and the first day in the city isn't spent getting everybody to relax and make up. Every mother knows how wearing it is on her patience to be listening to the constant whine of *"How much longer will it be?"* and *"I'm hungry and thirsty and tired!"* And that's just from Dad!

Let's spend the next few pages planning how we'll get to New York in a way that will not only make the trip as painless as possible, but also add to everybody's fun and excitement. It *can* be done! On a trip like this, attitude is everything. If everybody is excited about the trip, has helped plan it, knows what to expect, and sees it as a great adventure, even the often-tedious parts, like actually getting there, *can* be fun. (You might want to bookmark this page and read those last two sentences every night at the dinner table.)

Getting There

Let's dispose of the hardest issue first: What's the best way to get to New York City?

As far as I'm concerned, New York is worth getting to in any way you can. I'll never write a book about a place I *don't* like and wouldn't take my family. This is one of the most fabulous family destinations in the world, and my advice is to get there however you can, even if it means riding that circus elephant after all.

But there are more practical means. It depends on where you're coming from.

Visitors from the eastern United States and from southern Ontario and Quebec have the most choices. Those from much further away, however, will almost certainly have to fly. We'll start with that.

Flying to New York City
Let's list the advantages of flying. First, it's fast. Second—uh, never mind. That's about it: It's fast. Flying lacks the comfort of trains, the flexibility of cars, the inexpensiveness of the bus, and the novelty of elephant-back. But it's fast. And that means that people have less time to complain about the act of traveling and more time to enjoy the destination. The guy who said "Getting there is half the fun" obviously wasn't traveling halfway around the world by air with his family.

Flying with your family should be an adventure and if that's Mom and Dad's attitude, the kids will pick up on it quickly. There's lots to see in the airports, plenty of sights and sounds on the plane, excitement galore once you land. If you let kids know ahead of time just what to expect, they'll cope just fine, even if this is their first flight.

As it is with every other aspect of this trip, planning is the key. Parents who travel frequently with children have learned countless strategies for keeping their offspring companionable travel partners. Much depends on the kids' ages, of course. Teens cope as well as adults, although it's a good idea to review with them what will happen. Otherwise, they will do fine at entertaining themselves, for the most part.

Here are some of the best ideas I know for reducing the travel stress for kids of various ages.

Before the Trip: Let children know what to expect, especially if they've never flown before. If possible, drive to a nearby airport to watch people bustle around, get their tickets, check their bags. Go through the metal detector and put something through the scanner for carry-on bags, and stroll down the concourse watching people check in at the gates and board their planes. Watch people arriving, too, and point out how happy people are when they get to their destinations.

Walk around for awhile, pointing out toilets, restaurants, and shops so your children will know that anything they need will be available. Stand at the window (or on the observation deck if the airport has one) and watch planes leaving and arriving. Point out the trucks that carry the luggage, the food, the fuel, and how well everyone works together. Point out the control tower, where men and women keep an eye on everything, talk to the pilots, and make sure all the planes get in and out safely.

At home, talk about what airplanes are like inside, how there are plenty of toilets, the fact that on a long flight everyone will be served food right at their seats and that a movie or some TV shows might be shown on big screens, on television sets hanging from the ceiling, or on tiny screens on the back of the seat in front of them. Remind children that an airplane is noisy and sometimes a little bumpy, but that those are normal things.

The plane will be crowded and there won't be any room for them to get up and move around. It won't hurt to mention that the pilot and crew members are probably moms and dads, too, and want to do everything very safely so they can hurry home to their own families.

Warn everybody that there *will* be delays and they are usually because airports are very busy. Maybe the plane will board late or sit on the runway for awhile. That's part of air travel, unfortunately, but remind them that it's still a lot faster than driving for days across the country or swimming all the way across an ocean.

Also tell everybody what to expect when you arrive. If you're coming from another country you'll have to stand in the long immigration and customs lines. (Canadians can often take care of these formalities before they board the plane in Canada.) Finally there will be a tedious trip from the airport to your apartment or hotel. These things are presented in detail in the next chapter.

Kids—especially young ones—are not very flexible, and they'll deal more easily with the stresses of travel if they know what to expect.

At the Airport: Departure day will go smoothly if you've done your planning well. Whatever you do, allow plenty of time to make your flight. Rushing adds to everyone's stress level, and kids are the most susceptible. I don't like sitting in airports any more than you do, but I'm *always* annoyingly early for a flight, and that sometimes irritated our kids. On the other hand, I've noticed that since they became adults in charge of making their own travel arrangements, they leave for the airport every bit as early as I do.

Check your bags and stroll to your boarding gate. Stop along the way to buy mints or gum for everyone to keep their ears from feeling stuffed up on takeoff and landing. Buy everyone

one more magazine. But make sure you're early enough to take this slowly.

Besides the checked luggage, everyone will have his or her own carry-on bag. The kids' bags should be packed full of things to keep them busy for the rest of the day. The contents will vary depending on the age and interests of the child, but here are ideas:

Books and magazines are a must, and a book of puzzles can be fun and helps pass the time. Hand-held video games and tape or CD players are popular, and can be used throughout the trip, except at the very beginning or end. Make sure you have earphones so you don't disturb other passengers. You can't use a radio on the plane, though. A deck of cards or small travel games can be fun for two people sitting side-by-side, and you should have no trouble finding miniature chess and checker sets or scaled-down versions of well-known board games at toy stores or stores that sell travel supplies. A doll or stuffed animal will be a good friend for a small child. Every carry-on should hold an assortment of snacks and a drink. A kid never complains when his or her mouth is full!

While you're waiting to board, give the kids money to play some of the video games you'll certainly find nearby, and feeding them *always* works. Play people-watching games. Count the number of different sports-team hats or shirts people are wearing, or find the tee-shirt with the funniest saying. Carry a small folding map and find the cities that flights are going to or arriving from. Strategies like these will make the waiting (and the delays) more fun... or at least more bearable.

Finally, check at the desk to find out what time the flight will board. About ten minutes before that, have the kids visit the bathroom one more time. That way if takeoff is delayed after the plane has loaded, the kids won't be any more uncomfortable than necessary while they're stuck in their seats on the taxiway.

During the Trip: Once you're aloft the frantic pace of the airport disappears and there is nothing to do, maybe for endless hours, if you're coming from far away. If the kids will sleep, that's the very best way to pass the time, especially if you're on an overnight flight from somewhere. That's not always easy; not everyone sleeps well in cramped cabin conditions. During all of the hundreds of hours your intrepid author has spent aloft, I've slept exactly seventeen minutes. But kids will generally do better, especially if you can persuade them not to watch the movie on a long flight.

If the kids sit next to the window, they might be able to entertain themselves by watching the ground below, unless you're flying at night or it's cloudy. Even on a flight over the ocean, you can sometimes be lucky enough to spot a ship below on a clear day. At the very least, a window seat offers something to lean against and insulation from the traffic in the aisle, things that might be helpful if they do try to sleep.

Meals, if you're flying a long way, will take up part of the time. But the kids will have to dip into everything in their carry-ons eventually. Mom or Dad might carry a surprise—a book or game no one else knew was there—to bring out halfway through the flight. Feeding them *always* works.

Airplanes don't have much room to move around, but every 60 to 90 minutes, unless they're asleep, take a walk up and down the aisle with younger kids so they can stretch and move a little. You might find a little more room near the toilets, if there's no line, or near the galley.

Yes, traveling with children can be a character-building experience, but once you get where you're going, everyone will quickly shake off the dust of the journey. You've got a terrific time ahead of you.

For more about flying, including strategies for finding affordable airfares, see the sidebar *Getting a Fare Deal* in this chapter.

Getting a Fare Deal

The tax code of the United States, the decline and fall of the Roman Empire, and the Theory of Relativity—all of these, taken together—are easier to understand than the pricing systems used by the world's airlines. A few, to be sure, do have fare structures of fixed and consistent prices to specific destinations. But more often, passengers will have to thread their ways through a maze of prices and regulations that's harder than learning a foreign language—backwards!

There are tricks to getting the lowest fare, though, and whether you're using a travel agent or striking out on your own over the Web, you'll get a better deal if you know the secrets. These tips can cut your airline bill by 10 to 50 percent or more.

Travel during "Low Season." If you can avoid travel from May through September, you'll usually find lower prices (except at Christmas). If you're coming from outside North America, the best deals are usually between mid-November and mid-March. Of course there are drawbacks. Weather is less pleasant and attractions are sometimes open fewer hours, but a winter trip might be possible even when a summer trip would increase the cost of the holiday too much.

Avoid flying on weekends. Prices often are 5 to 10 percent higher on Friday, Saturday, and Sunday. Fly midweek and save.

Stay at least a week. The best rates are frequently offered for stays of between 7 and 30 days. Business travelers like short stays, and airlines squeeze as much as they can from corporate travelers. A Saturday-night stay is almost always essential for getting the best fare.

Check prices at all nearby airports. Prices can vary by 25 percent and more between airports just an hour's drive apart. If you're lucky enough to have several airports to choose among, you'll almost certainly find different prices at some of them. The closest might be the cheapest—or it might not be.

Check prices for all three NYC airports. Prices can vary by a surprising amount. If you're coming from abroad, you might find a flight to Newark cheaper than one to JFK.

Be willing to make connections. It makes no sense, of course, but we've sometimes found that it's cheaper to drive to an airport 50 miles from our home and take a flight that originates there, flies to our hometown, and then goes on to our destination, than to simply take the flight directly from home. Crazy. Non-stop flights usually cost more, simply because people are willing to pay more for them.

Check out consolidators. These are companies that buy blocks of tickets from airlines and resell them at prices lower than the airlines charge individual customers. They advertise in the travel sections of large Sunday newspapers. A travel agent can help steer you toward the most reliable consolidators.

Look for frequent flier deals. Some airlines offer big mileage bonuses to new members. Taking a whole family on a trip might yield enough miles to qualify for a free ticket or two for your next trip.

Watch for sales. Airlines have sales just like any other business. If you buy tickets at a higher price, they will normally credit you with the difference, less a service fee. Here, too, a travel agent can keep an eye open for you, because the agent checks prices every day, something you probably won't do after you've bought your tickets.

There's no way to guarantee that you've paid the lowest price on the plane. But these rules will put you ahead of the game. An airline's job is to get as much money as it can out of you; your job is to pay as little as possible. These tips will at least help shift the odds a bit more in your favor.

Taking the Train

This is no option if you're coming from another country except Canada, of course, but if you're already in the United States, it might be a possibility. For most Americans living west of Philadelphia, the suggestion of taking a train will be met with the same skepticism that would greet a proposal that they travel by elephant. It's not really possible, and even if it were, why would anyone want to?

For several reasons.

• Trains are more comfortable.

• Railway stations (where they exist) are often more accessible than airports and might even feature free parking.

• Railway stations are less busy and crowded and have none of the security measures necessary at airports—no one tries to hijack a train.

• Trains deliver you to the heart of Manhattan, not at an airport miles from where you want to be.

• Train food is better than airplane food.

• Trains are at least as likely to arrive on time as airplanes.

• A train's departure is never delayed by weather.

• The view from a train is never obscured by clouds.

• Trains usually cost less than planes, often *much* less.

There's one big drawback, though: If you're coming from much more than about 100 miles away, trains take longer.

For most people that's decisive, even if they live in an area of the country that is served by Amtrak, the national long-haul passenger service in the United States. Still, the train is worth considering if it's not too inconvenient and if you'd like to begin your holiday with something a bit different. Kids love trains and if your trip involves overnight travel, they're more likely to sleep on a train than they would have on an airplane.

Amtrak serves hundreds of cities along its main rail corridors. Starting from both Ohio and Connecticut, we've sometimes driven to one of those smaller stations, where parking is free, to catch a train to New York or Washington, and have enjoyed the relaxed pace of train travel. Where time is not an issue, we much prefer it to flying or driving.

A few examples might be in order. From Orlando there are two trains a day to New York City, taking about 20 hours. The train from Atlanta takes 18 hours, and the two direct trains a day from Chicago take 20 hours. All are overnight trips but, unlike seats on airplanes, even the coach seats are roomy and comfortable for sleeping.

The roughly 30 trains a day from Washington, D.C. take about 3 hours and the 10 from Boston just 4 or 5 hours.

Those are perfectly practical itineraries even for families. Prices are no more than airfare, and Amtrak seems always to be running a variety of promotions and discounts that pull the price down. From further away, though, you might have to spend two, even three nights on the train and while Amtrak does offer nice family bedrooms, that can greatly inflate the cost of the trip.

Trains arrive at Penn Station in the heart of Manhattan, less than two blocks from the Empire State Building and only steps from eleven different subway lines. Getting from the train station to your accommodations, wherever they are, will be as easy as it ever can be in New York City.

Driving

I've driven in New York City, and I've had surgery. I'm not sure which of those experiences I enjoyed the most.

Okay, that's an untrue and unfair exaggeration. Millions of people *do* drive in the city and it's really no more difficult than driving in any other large city. If you plan where you're going, look at a map before you leave, have a good navigator, and can keep your cool, you'll be able to get everywhere, except perhaps at rush hour, when you probably won't get anywhere.

Finding a place to park when you get there is another matter.

The movies and TV shows we've all seen, where the hero drives up a lightly-traveled street and parks right in front of the building he's going to—pure fiction! Parking is non-existent anywhere near the places you want to go, unless you're willing to pay astronomical prices. You can easily pay more to park your car for a week in New York City than a plane ticket would cost.

Why do New Yorkers even have cars? Many don't. When one of our sons moved to the city, almost the first thing he did was to sell his car. His exact words were, "I need a car in New York about as much as I need a camel." You can travel everywhere on the subway for about $1.50. Driving will take you longer than going on the subway, you'll park further away from your destination than the nearest station, and you'll pay $8 an hour for the privilege.

What about driving to the city and leaving your car in the hotel garage? That works, but the hotel will charge $20 to $30 per day, maybe more.

If you've rented an apartment outside Manhattan, free street parking is possible, although it might be hard to find close to your apartment. You'll have to move your car a couple of days a

week, as well, to give street cleaners room to work. Streets are posted about what days parking is prohibited on each side of the street, and violators will be ticketed or towed.

Parking *is* easier for some of the attractions outside Manhattan... but not enough to make the hassle and expense of a car worthwhile for the rest of the trip.

Unless your hotel or apartment provides inexpensive, secure parking (something, to be fair, that another of

Traffic can be intimidating to a newcomer

our kids *did* have during the ten months he lived in Queens), bringing your car to the city isn't worth the cost or aggravation.

If driving is the only way you can afford this trip, here's a compromise solution. Drive to the greater New York area, park your car outside the

> ***Tip:*** If you're undeterred, avoid rush hour and have a good street map of all five boroughs. Auto clubs publish them but the type is tiny and they open up to the size of bedsheets. City street atlases are hard to find outside the city but your local bookstore should be able to order the 5 Borough Pocketatlas from the Geographia Map Company or the NY@tlas from VanDam, Inc.

city, and take public transportation into Manhattan. You'll find free or inexpensive parking near many railway stations in New Jersey, in Connecticut, or in parts of New York state well north of the city, and can take advantage of Amtrak or inexpensive commuter rail services into the city.

Amtrak, which has stops in places like Princeton and New Brunswick, NJ, is a good choice for drivers coming from the south. New York City's Metropolitan Transit Authority (MTA) runs commuter rail lines to dozens of places as far out as Waterbury, CT; Mahwah, NJ; and Middletown, NY, to the north and east. Round-trip fares for the whole family will come to less than one or two days' parking at a Midtown garage, and a *lot* less than the cost of getting your illegally-parked car returned from the police impound lot.

Packing for the Trip

If you've decided to drive, packing isn't much of a problem—you can take two of everything. But if you're traveling by air or rail, you're limited to how much you can carry. Here are the Ten Commandments of packing.

• Remember that unless the weather is very warm indeed, it's perfectly okay for people to wear the same clothes more than once. Few people you encounter on this trip will care about the extent of your wardrobe and if they do, well, you'll probably never see them again anyway.

• Take neat but comfortable clothes. You'll be welcomed everywhere, except in a handful of restaurants you can't afford to take a whole family anyway. If you like, take one dressier outfit if you're planning something special, but dressing up will seldom be expected.

• Think *layers*. Weather can be broiling hot or utterly frigid. (Natives will claim you can get both in the same afternoon.)

• Stick to one basic color and its complements. Then anything can be worn with anything else.

• Don't skimp on comfortable shoes with good support. Everyone will walk a lot more than they usually do and a person with sore feet is a cranky person.

• If you're staying for more than a week, don't try to carry enough clothes for the whole trip. Spend one afternoon or evening at the launderette, or wash out a few things by hand every day or two.

Remember that you have more clothes than you think: You have the clothes you're traveling in!

• If you're coming from outside North America, leave electrical appliances at home unless they're dual voltage. A power transformer that works well will cost more than a new hair drier or electric razor in the city. In fact, it's easier to leave that stuff at home even if you're only coming from New Jersey.

• If you forget something you *really* need, remember that New York has several stores. Chances are you can buy it there. Call it a souvenir.

• A good rule of thumb is to take half of what you think you'll need. To check yourself, pack your suitcase and take it for a walk. If you can carry it for half a mile (almost 1 km) without setting it down, congratulations! You're a champion packer.

Suitcases

If you're flying or taking the train, don't take more than one suitcase for every two people. That will keep everybody from overpacking, it will give each person a partner to help carry the bag, and it

> *Tip:* *If you're flying, get two rolls of brightly colored plastic tape and put a simple design on each side of each bag, and a couple of tape strips around each handle. A lot of suitcases look alike and the tape will help you spot yours on the baggage carrousel, and signal other travelers with similar bags that those are yours!*

will make it easier to get around airports and train stations.

Unless you're toting fragile items, soft-sided bags are best because they're much lighter. We've got a lightweight nylon bag that folds up to almost nothing that we carry in the bottom of one suitcase as well. If we're coming home with a lot of souvenirs, we have an extra suitcase without going over our baggage allowance.

Carry-on Bags

We associate carry-ons with flying, but they're great for any sort of travel. Each member of the family should have his or her own—no need to share this time. A carry-on needn't be fancy; a backpack, a canvas tote that snaps or zips shut, a small overnight bag—these are all you need.

If you're flying, everyone should have a change of clothes in his or her bag. It doesn't happen often, but sometimes one of your suitcases will go off on a holiday of its own and takes an extra day to catch up with you. Medicines, film, money, tickets, and other travel documents should never be in checked baggage. We discussed some ideas for the contents of the kids' bags a few pages ago.

The Joy of Travel

We've never bought much in the way of souvenirs on our journeys: small, inexpensive items like candles or tapes of local music, a miniature painting—that's about it. The mementos that are most precious to the Lains, usually, are our photographs and journals.

You don't need a fancy camera to take great pictures in New York City; it's a very photogenic place. But if you're flying there, protect your film! The people who operate the scanners at airports will always tell you their equipment will not harm film. It will! All three of the world's major film manufacturers—Kodak, Fuji, and Agfa—recommend strongly that your film be hand inspected, *not* passed through the scanner. High-speed films can be ruined in a single exposure.

Airport personnel are supposed to hand inspect film on request, but when they're busy, they often resist. For about $20 at most camera stores you can buy a lead-lined bag that will protect your film from the x-rays used to inspect carry-on bags. Don't put your film in your checked luggage, though, even in one of those lead bags. Scanners used for checked luggage are much more powerful and will ruin even protected film. Keep it in your carry-on.

The day you start your trip, give everybody a notebook and a pen. The only souvenirs that are as precious to me as my photos are my travel journals. I'm not very reliable at keeping a diary otherwise, but I'm good about it when I travel, and rereading those pages can make a trip come alive for me years later. Kids often resist the idea, but if they spend just ten minutes a day jotting their thoughts, they'll be *so* glad they did later, even if they won't admit it. Encourage them to write down what they had to eat each day, what the weather was like, what the neatest and most boring thing was they saw every day, what surprised them most, what they thought was most exciting. The journal will be a treasured keepsake. And assure them that all journals are private—their thoughts will remain their own.

Recommendations

✔ Let inexperienced travelers know what to expect; they'll be more content and be better companions.

✔ Everyone should have his or her own carry-on, filled with necessities and things to do.

✔ When all else fails, feed people. You can't carry too many snacks. Traveling is hungry work.

✔ Make the process of getting to New York as stress-free as possible. Leave plenty of time for everything and concentrate on relaxing. This is supposed to be fun!

4. Arrival!

We're here! After all the planning, all the anticipation, all the inconvenience of moving a family from one point on the planet to another, you're actually in New York City! Now what?

That's going to depend on just how you got here and where you came from. First let's get you to your apartment or hotel, and then I'll offer some travel-tested advice on what to do when you get there. You're eager to get through the formalities of travel and arrival and start seeing the sights you've been anticipating. Just have a little more patience and in another couple of hours at the most, you'll be ready to take your first bite of the Big Apple.

Arrival by Automobile

Chapter 3 suggested that you leave your car at home. If you drove anyway, however, please don't arrive at rush hour. New York City transport authorities define rush hour as 6:30 to 9:30 A.M. and 3:30 to 8 P.M. The traffic, which is always bad, is at its worst then. Your best bet is usually to arrive at midday or in the late evening.

Arrival!

Any good highway map will show you the main arteries into the city and which one you choose will depend on the direction you're driving from and where you're going. Stick to the expressways for as long as you can, switching to surface streets only when you get near your destination.

For example, if you're staying in Manhattan and coming from the north, the best route might be the Franklin D. Roosevelt Parkway (FDR) along the East River, but to the west side of Brooklyn from the north you'll probably come down I-87 or I-278 and follow the Brooklyn-Queens Expressway (BQE) to the Gowanus Expressway or Ocean Parkway. From other directions and to other parts of the city your route will be different, so a good map is indispensable. Be aware that most bridges and tunnels into the city charge a toll.

When you leave the expressway, switch to a more detailed atlas and have your route marked out in advance, so your navigator doesn't have to figure out the route and direct the driver at the same time. Patience is essential for driving in New York City (even if the natives seem especially *im*patient) and

Try to avoid driving during rush hour

| |
| **Tip:** The Port Authority garage has 1,000 parking spaces, but it's popular with commuters. If you arrive during the day, you might need to park in a more expensive facility until night, then move your car to the garage when the commuters have gone home. |

adding another fifteen minutes to your drive by taking it calmly is fifteen minutes well spent.

Parking? Consult the hotel or apartment landlord for advice. In the boroughs, street parking might be available, although there will be plenty of competition for it.

Some travelers park their cars in the long-term lots at LaGuardia or Kennedy airports and rely on public transportation. At LaGuardia, long-term parking in Lot 3 near the USAirways terminal costs about $25 for the first day but just $10 per day thereafter. Nearby long-term lots cost about $15 per day if the official LaGuardia lot is full. At Kennedy the rate is about $10 per day.

If you decide on that option, go down to the Air Arrival section in this chapter to learn about public transportation from the airports.

If you're looking for the most reasonable parking in central Manhattan, consider the Port Authority Bus Terminal garage at 42nd Street and Eighth Avenue at about $22 per day. This is especially convenient for drivers arriving from the west, since a ramp from the Lincoln Tunnel leads directly to the garage and there's no need to confront Manhattan traffic. Eleven subway lines run within a block of the garage.

Arrival by Train

Amtrak, PATH trains from New Jersey, and Long Island Rail trains arrive at Penn Station (33rd Street and Eighth Avenue). Thirteen subway lines converge near here and there's a taxi rank outside the station.

Most other commuter trains arrive at Grand Central Terminal

at 42nd Street and Park Avenue. Here are four subway lines (plus the S train which shuttles riders to Times Square) and taxi ranks. Getting to your lodgings from either station will give you your first taste of authentic New York City.

Arrival by Air

There are three major airports serving New York City: *LaGuardia (LGA)*, which handles domestic and some Canadian flights; *John F. Kennedy International (JFK)*, America's busiest international gateway; and *Newark International (EWR)* in New Jersey, which also handles both domestic and international traffic.

International Arrivals

First of all, make sure you know the visa rules for visiting the United States. The nearest American embassy or consulate can help you, or you can go to the Immigration Service website listed at the end of the book for information. Tourists from 26 countries, including much of Western Europe, Japan, Australia, and New Zealand are able to enter the U.S. for up to 90 days without a visa. Everyone else must obtain a visa before they arrive.

If you are arriving from outside North America (Canadian passengers can often go through these steps before boarding their plane in Canada), you'll receive a landing card (form I-94) from your flight attendant before your plane lands. (This will always be provided on the plane. Don't pay to order one over the Web.) Here you will provide your name, flight number, where and how long you're staying, and some additional information about what you're bringing into the country with you. Fill out the card and keep it with your passport and, if applicable, visa.

Once you land, your next hour or so is completely out of your control. All you need to do is to follow the throng of people from place to place. But all the hiking you'll do in clearing customs and immigration will be great practice for the walking you'll do seeing the sights of New York, so you might as well enjoy it.

> **Tip:** *Make sure you've got a bit of food handy, like nuts or granola bars. It takes awhile to get to your accommodations from the airports in New York, and people whose stomachs are growling are more likely to growl themselves.*

First stop will be Immigration. Your family should go up to the booth together. Have your papers ready when you reach the inspector, where your I-94 form, passports, and visas if you have them, will be inspected and stamped. Immigration officials have a fearsome reputation, and none more so than those at JFK. But I'll be honest: I've never been greeted with anything but politeness. Have your paperwork ready, answer the simple questions they might ask ("Are you here for business or pleasure?" is the most common), and smile: It will surprise them.

Next stop will be the baggage carousels, and when you've claimed your luggage (one of your suitcases will be the last one off the plane—count on it) just follow the crowd to Customs. Unless you're bringing in products you intend to sell, you can follow the green line, *Nothing to Declare*. It's possible that an inspector will ask to see the contents of your bags, but unlikely. Walk through the doors at the end of Customs and you're *really* in the United States of America at last.

Now follow the signs that say *Ground Transportation* and skip to the section below, *Getting in from the Airport*.

Domestic Arrivals

If you're coming from somewhere in the United States, or on many flights from Canada, the process is much less complicated, since you won't have to bother with Immigration and Customs. Get off the plane, get your bags, and follow the *Ground Transportation* signs near the baggage carousel. It won't be long now!

Arrival!

Getting in from the Airport

I truly like New York. It's one of the most exciting and diverse cities in the world and almost anything that's available anywhere in the world is available in New York City. Almost anything. Almost.

Anything except decent airport transportation.

Most of the world's great cities, and a lot of mediocre ones, too, have fast, convenient trains on dedicated lines that run straight from the airport to the center city. If only that were true here! There's been a lot of talk over the years about constructing new rail lines to serve air travelers, but it hasn't happened so far. JFK isn't as bad as LaGuardia or Newark, because at least the regular subway is easily accessible by shuttle bus. And Newark has a bus to the PATH train that's not too bad. But neither is as convenient or as fast as many other cities are able to boast.

But if that's the worst thing about a trip to New York (and it might be), that's not such a terrible fault. Millions of people a year fly into New York, so it must be possible to manage. Just plan your route ahead of time, and if you have any questions, ask the people who know—the people at the transportation booth.

Each airport has a Transportation Information counter located in the baggage claim area of each terminal. Personnel there can advise you on the fastest, cheapest, or easiest way to get to your destination. I can't possibly list all the options here, although the airport websites listed at the end of the book have extensive information. Here's a summary of the most common ways people come in from the airport.

From LaGuardia

USAirways and Delta Air Lines have their own terminals at LGA; all other flights use the central terminal building. All transportation options are available at each terminal.

Taxi: There are taxi stands available outside each terminal. Fare to upper or midtown Manhattan will be about $25, not including tolls and tip, which will push the total to $30 or more. Fares to Queens, Brooklyn, or lower Manhattan will be between $10 and $40, depending on the distance. The taxi dispatcher at each stand can give you an estimated charge.

Bus: To Manhattan, the cheapest option is the city bus, which costs just $1.50. The M60 bus stops at each terminal and goes across 125th Street on Manhattan's north side, terminating at 106th Street near Columbia University. You can transfer to the subway at several places along 125th Street.

For about $10 per person you can take a New York Airport Express Service bus directly to the Port Authority bus terminal on 42nd Street in Midtown. There are numerous other bus services as well.

Subway: For destinations in Manhattan, Brooklyn, and Queens, the subway is an inexpensive choice. Go to the city bus stop in front of your terminal and look for a Q33 bus. They come about every 30 minutes. Fare is $1.50, exact change only (no dollar bills accepted). Ride the bus to the Jackson Heights-

LaGuardia is a clean, easy airport to navigate

Arrival!

Roosevelt Avenue stop (Ask your driver to alert you) where you can transfer to the subway system. Subway lines 7, E, F, and R cover Queens and Manhattan, and line G cuts through Queens and down into Brooklyn. You might need to transfer once to get close to where you want to be.

This seems terribly complicated, but every member of the Lain clan can attest that it's easier than it sounds. You won't get lost and you'll get a close-up introduction to New York City. The No. 7 subway has a great view of midtown, guaranteed to excite the kids, as it runs along its elevated tracks in Queens.

From Kennedy Airport

JFK has nine terminal buildings. The website listed in the back of the book can tell you which of the almost 90 airlines that serve JFK arrive at which terminals. A free shuttle bus connects the terminals. All transportation options are available at all terminals or within minutes via the shuttle. Everything at JFK is well marked.

Taxi: There are taxi stands available outside each terminal. Fare to Midtown Manhattan will be about $30, not including tolls and tip. Fares to Queens, Brooklyn, or Lower Manhattan will be between $15 and $40, depending on the distance. The taxi dispatcher at each stand can give you an estimated charge.

Bus: You can't take a regular city bus from JFK to Manhattan. There are none. A Trans-Bridge bus to the Port Authority terminal costs about $10 and the New York Airport Express Service bus is about $13. Check with the Transportation Information counter or see the website for other options.

Subway: The free shuttle bus will take you to the subway station at Howard Beach, where you can catch the A train that cuts through the north side of Brooklyn and runs up the full length of Manhattan, all the way to 207th Street. The fare is just $1.50. It's a long ride, but you cross almost every other line in the system and one transfer can take you anywhere in the city.

From Newark International

EWR has three terminals connected by monorail. Most domestic flights use Terminals A and C, while international flights normally use Terminal B. All transportation options are available at all terminals or within minutes via the monorail.

Taxi: There are taxi stands available outside each terminal. Fare to Manhattan will be about $40 plus tolls and tip. To Queens or Brooklyn you'll probably pay $50 to $60. The taxi dispatcher at each stand can give you an estimated charge.

Bus: The Olympia Airport Express bus to the Port Authority terminal or Grand Central costs about $11. Check with the Transportation Information counter for services to the other boroughs, or see the website for other options.

Train: The subway doesn't run out here, but the PATH train does. Take a New Jersey Transit Airlink bus (No. 302) to the train station. You'll need exact change for the bus ($4) and the train ($1). The train makes several stops in Lower Manhattan, ending at Penn Station.

At Home in New York City

Before I go to a new city for the first time, I'm completely absorbed in the planning: Reading everything I can about the place. Arranging accommodations. Pumping up the enthusiasm of my traveling companions. Planning itineraries. Consulting maps and guidebooks. Working out my budget. My family says I'm compulsive. I prefer to think of it as thorough.

At last, after all the planning and anticipation, I'm finally there and my reaction is always the same: *Panic!*

I get so wrapped up in planning a trip that, once I'm actually at my destination I feel this sudden surge of pressure to rush out, see everything, and do everything so all that preliminary work can start to pay off.

Fortunately over the years I've learned to put this compulsion aside and take it slowly. That's easier for parents to do than kids, though. If you spend the first few hours of your visit getting organized and setting a relaxed pace, your entire trip is likely to be well organized and relaxed. If those important first hours are hurried and stressful, on the other hand, you (and especially the kids!) are more likely to feel rushed and frazzled for the next week or two. This is a vacation, maybe the best one you've ever taken—you don't need stress!

Everyone is eager to get out and do what they came for—sightseeing. But for the first few hours in the city, follow the advice below. You'll thank me for it later. Remember this axiom of travel: *The mood of the group is determined by its most tired member.* Every parent knows this. Keep it in mind today.

So how should you spend your first few hours in New York?

First: Move in and unpack—Unpacking is a chore and people often put it off for as long as possible. Know this: Later you'll feel even less like unpacking than you do now. Get this chore out of the way first; otherwise you'll feel it hanging over your head for the rest of the day.

Second: (Maybe) take a nap—This is the hardest advice in the book. But wait: It might not apply to you! *If* you've arrived in New York after an overnight flight, perhaps from the western United States, or from Asia or Australia, this step is essential and you omit it at the risk of a three-day jet lag. Traveling west to east is harder on the body than going the other way. Everyone should take a nap of two to three hours (not more, however, no matter how tired you are) and go to bed at the usual time tonight. If you do, you'll wake up in the morning with your body clock readjusted and will feel fine for the rest of the trip. Omit it and you'll feel like a zombie for two or three days.

If you've had a long daytime flight across three or more time zones, a nap is less essential. But take it easy today anyway. Your body is out of kilter and it will take a good night's sleep tonight to set it right. Everyone should go to bed at their regular time and they'll feel fine in the morning.

Third: Explore your neighborhood—If you're really going to Live Like a Local, you want to see what your new home is like. This is a good way to ease into the sightseeing mode. You'll be shopping where your neighbors shop, eating at local restaurants, doing your laundry where the person in the next apartment does hers, using the nearby subway stations and bus stops to get around. This neighborhood will be your home for the next week or two; get to know it! Where's the best place to get fresh bagels in the morning? Where can you buy a newspaper? Is there a local ice cream shop for late-night treats? A pizza place where you can get great slabs of delicious New York style pies? A local park where you can relax after hours of walking? A deli that makes thick pastrami sandwiches? A 24-hour market for the time you run out of eggs?

In New York City, all those places will be within a block or two of wherever you're staying. If you find them the first afternoon you're in the city, you'll be able to take advantage of them throughout your stay.

Take a walk around your neighborhood to get acquainted with the area

This is also a good time to stop by the nearest subway station and buy your MetroCards, if you haven't already done so. Stretching your legs after hours of travel is just what everyone needs to get a

> *Tip:* *Before you leave home, make an enlarged photocopy of the map of your neighborhood for every member of your family who's old enough to read it. On your first-day walk, have them mark all the places they might want to return to.*

new surge of energy. One word of warning, though. If you've had a flight of more than three or four hours, go a little easy on the walking today. Your feet swell in the pressurized cabin of an airplane because you don't move around much, and if you overdo the walking today you risk raising blisters that will cause you considerable grief for the next week.

Fourth: Eat—The Lains have never had any trouble following *this* advice! And it's perfect to combine with the neighborhood exploration. You're bound to come across several places to eat, and by now, everyone's hungry. It's close to lunch or dinner time now, so don't put it off. Add some more fuel to the furnace and stop at that Peruvian restaurant down the street, the gyro place in the next block, or the Thai buffet across from the park. New York is filled with every type of cuisine imaginable and while sometimes the kids will want to have favorite dishes, you should encourage them to try new things, too. Today is a perfect opportunity to do that. *Everything* is new today.

Fifth: Shop for basics—If you're staying in an apartment, this is the time to stock up on some groceries for the meals you plan to fix, and other supplies you might need. Stick to simple, easy-to-prepare foods. No one will feel like standing in the kitchen fixing something complicated after a long day of walking. Even if you're staying in a hotel, you're much better off buying soft drinks and snacks at the local market than in the hotel, where they're sure to cost twice as much. In fact, even in a hotel you can keep fruit, cereal, and other simple items for breakfast.

Sixth: Do a little sightseeing—If everybody's up to it and it's not too late, this is the time to go see something. If it's evening already and you're in Brooklyn, a stroll along the promenade is a great end to your first day, with the Manhattan skyline lit up storybook fashion for your personal viewing pleasure. If you're in upper or midtown Manhattan you might want to go to Times Square and soak in the bright lights and vibrant atmosphere. If you're in lower Manhattan, Battery Park City with its spectacular views of skyscrapers to the east and New York Harbor and the Statue of Liberty to the west can't be beat. If you've arrived early in the day and have plenty of time, you couldn't have a better first day than by taking the Lain Walking Tour in Chapter 6.

Remember, though, if you've had hard traveling, don't overdo it today. You've got plenty of time and you can't experience everything this city has to offer no matter how long you stay. Tomorrow, when everyone is well rested and has had their first night's sleep in the city that never does—then you can shift into high gear. We're here, and New York awaits us!

Recommendations

✔ If you're driving, plan your route into the city carefully and arrive at midday or late evening. If you arrive by air, check the Web pages in the back of the book for the best route to your accommodations.

✔ If you've had an overnight flight, take a nap. You need it, even if you don't think you do.

✔ Don't try to do everything on your list the first day. If you wear yourself out or raise blisters today, you'll be sorry tomorrow. Build up to it.

5. Food, New York Style

Think about it: Here is a city of 8 million people and not *one* of them produces a scrap of food for anyone else. Every morsel has to be brought in from some other place! Do you have any idea how many people that is? Line 'em up, end to end, and they'll reach from New York City to the Pacific Ocean. And back again. And almost back to the Pacific again, finally petering out somewhere in the Rocky Mountains. And that's not even counting the million or so visitors in the city each day!

Yet somehow, each and every one of those millions of people gets fed. Not just a little bit, but for most of them pretty much all they want, three meals a day with nibbles and snacks whenever they feel the urge. Heaps of food! Mountains of food! All of it arriving on trucks, trains, airplanes, ships, and for all I know, on elephant-back, 24 hours a day. Keeping a major city fed is one of the true marvels of the modern world, and my head spins whenever I think about it: I just cannot conceive of how it's possible.

A few world cities are larger than New York, but nowhere else, I think, has such a great quantity and unrivaled variety of food. If you like to eat, you ought to enjoy New York City. Let's spend a few pages talking about how to keep your family fed and happy. They do seem to go together—at least our family was always happiest when being fed.

Mealtime Strategies

Food will be one of your three major expenses (along with accommodations and travel to New York) but there's a lot you can do to economize without stinting. Remember that even native New Yorkers eat inexpensive meals most of the time and if they can, so can you!

One of the reasons this book urges you to stay in an apartment rather than in a hotel is so you can save money by becoming a temporary New Yorker, living the way the locals do, instead of the way tourists do. In an apartment you can prepare some of your own meals, just the way you do at home, and save your dollars for other things.

Eating in Your Apartment

While it's true that New Yorkers eat out more than most other Americans, they still eat at home more often than not. It's usually quicker, often more convenient, and always cheaper to buy simple ingredients and prepare basic meals at home. If you want to Live Like a Local, that's what you'll do.

Don't expect to see vast supermarkets in midtown Manhattan. Many people, wherever they live in the city, don't own cars, and can't fill the trunk with countless sacks of groceries. City people shop more frequently and in smaller quantities, often just picking up enough for a day or two at a convenient market in the neighborhood. That's the perfect strategy for a visitor. You'll find a choice of small markets and grocery stores everywhere in the city, and you can pick up easy-to-prepare foods, all your beverages, and probably fresh produce within a block of where you're staying.

Breakfasts are cheap and easy to prepare, so that's a good start on saving time and money. Whether you prefer cereal and toast or eggs and bacon, the price of the fixings will be a fraction of what a restaurant breakfast will cost.

Lunches will usually be eaten on the go, and that's a subject for later in the chapter. But at the end of a day of sightseeing, everyone will enjoy the chance to go back to the apartment, take off their shoes, and collapse on the nearest piece of soft furniture before having a home-cooked supper. The Lains have found very few restaurants that welcome customers who take off their shoes and sprawl on the furniture.

A couple of points are really important here. First, everybody is tired at the end of a busy day, so be fair: *Everybody* should share meal duty. Maybe Mom cooked last night and today Dad will fix dinner. Tomorrow the oldest kids will be in charge. This probably works better than everybody pitching in together each day, because apartment kitchens are apt to be cramped. Experienced parents know what happens next when tired people start getting in each other's way....

Second, keep meals simple. Eat what you'd have at home. Kids, especially, will appreciate familiar meals after a day of being bombarded with new sights and experiences. But save the fancy, kitchen-intensive recipes for when you get home after your trip. It's no fun for the cook-of-the-day to spend an hour fixing a fancy dinner at the end of a 10-hour day of sightseeing.

This is one of the greatest money-saving strategies in the entire book. For $10 at the local grocery store, you can get everything you need to fix a tasty, uncomplicated supper for your *entire* family that's identical to the one you could buy at a restaurant down the street for $12 *per person*!

Eating in Your Hotel
If you're staying in a hotel, though, the best way to save money is to follow the Universal Rule of Hotel Dining:
DON'T!

There's not a gram of food sold *in* a hotel that's not available *outside* the hotel for much less money. That applies to everything from full dinner in the rooftop restaurant to a simple Danish and coffee from the coffee shop to a candy bar in the gift shop. Whatever you want to eat, a hotel is an expensive place to buy it.

The cheapest hotel breakfasts are the ones you provide yourself. Somewhere within a block of wherever you're staying you'll find a small bakery. Send somebody out to pick up fresh bagels, donuts, or pastries, coffee, and fruit juice. That's plenty to get everybody's engine started. Or look for one of the hundreds of corner markets: There's one on every street. Here you can get small boxes of cereal and a pint of milk. You can get everything you need for a quick breakfast for the entire family for less than $10—an amount that probably won't feed two people in the hotel coffee shop.

If you want something more elaborate, you'll have no trouble finding a coffee shop or diner within a block of your hotel where you can get eggs, pancakes, sausage—all the traditional breakfast items—for half of what you'd have to pay at the hotel.

Lunch on the Run

Lunch will seldom be an elaborate meal. You're probably in the middle of sightseeing and will be refueling, not dining. So when you get to the first stop of the day—a museum, park, or attraction—pay attention to what's available in the area before you begin. Major museums usually have restaurants on site. And you'll pay dearly to eat in them—cafeteria-style food at premium prices. You can do better.

From time to time I talk about the 2-Hour Rule: Never spend more than two hours at a single attraction. If you're following that advice, lunch will probably come after your first stop of the day, or maybe after the second.

The trick for finding a good place for lunch is to look for

someplace to eat *before* people get hungry… and therefore cranky and impatient.

Here's a tactic that's usually successful:

When you get close to

> ## *Tip:* *Always carry "iron rations" on your excursions. A granola bar, package of trail mix, or stick of beef jerky can stem the hunger pangs for an extra 30 minutes and keep everyone content and friendly.*

each destination, have everybody take a good look around, paying particular attention to places to eat. Make your decision *before* you enter the museum, park, or building. At this point, everyone is still fresh and good-humored and not in a hurry.

Two hours later you can simply walk back with no fuss to the place you selected. If a better idea has come up in the meantime, your group can always change its mind, but this way, at least, there's a clear choice to fall back on.

Most people will probably want to grab lunch from one of the ubiquitous fast-food franchises that clutter the world's cities: hamburgers, chicken, tacos—you know what I mean. That's okay. But there are better choices where the flavors of New York are not so filtered through the homogenizing effects of big corporations.

For starters, you could buy lunch from one of the hundreds of pushcarts that you'll find in every corner of the city. The sidebar "Pushing It" introduces you to the cuisine (if that's the word) that's as much a part of New York City as the Empire State Building.

For a real New York treat, have pizza. Not from one of the chains! Stop in one of the genuine local pizza parlors, like *Ray's* (outlets everywhere). This is nothing like what you're used to, unless you're visiting from Italy. The pies are already made, sitting on the counter. Just specify the toppings you want and they'll be added to a huge slice, popped back in the oven, and heated until the cheese is bubbling hot. One slice will be plenty, except for a teen going through a growth spurt. Eat it like a real

New Yorker, folding it in half lengthwise and downing it one-handed. Now that's Living Like a Local! Your lunch will be tastier, cheaper, and more filling than the burger and fries down the street.

Prefer a sandwich? This is the place to go for it! There's a deli in every neighborhood, often several. Small grocery stores might have deli counters, too. Just walk right up and read the list of sandwiches on the board behind the counter. Choose from corned beef, roast beef, pastrami, chicken, turkey, ham, salami, egg salad, chicken salad, tuna salad, ham salad, chopped liver, a half dozen varieties of cheese, and more. Have them by themselves or in combination on a choice of white, wheat, light rye, dark rye, onion roll, bagel, croissant, or who-knows-what-else. Make sure the man throws in a big pickle, grab a bag of chips and a soda, and you have the archetype of the New York lunch. Soups are a good bet, too.

Deli counters are always crowded at lunchtime and customers don't line up politely as they do in some other places. But don't be shy. Just wade into the crowd and work your way to the front

You can find a snack or a meal in parks or streets all over the city from the ubiquitous pushcarts

and shout out your order. That's Living Like a Local.

You can eat your sandwiches there (unless it's a deli counter in a grocery store, which might not have tables) but it's more fun to take your lunch and head for the nearest park or convenient bench, where you can watch the crowds passing by. The only way you could feel more like an authentic New Yorker would be to have a cell phone implanted in your ear.

All delis are not created equal. The famous ones are often worse. There's a big deli, well known to all visitors, in Times Square. Sandwiches there cost as much as a full steak dinner outside of New York, and the sandwiches are indeed huge. But even that teen on a growth spurt can't

Pushing It

You want food? You can buy about anything from soup to nuts from New York's many street vendors.

No, that's not a cliché—you really can! One windy March afternoon I stopped for a bowl of potato soup (one of four kinds on offer) from a street vendor at 48th Street and Avenue of the Americas, then picked up some warm honey-roasted pecans from the pushcart next to him.

In every borough of the city… in every fair-sized park… at every large intersection you'll find corner stands selling danishes, bagels, and coffee in the mornings and an enticing and aromatic array of other things throughout the day: sausages smothered in onions, hot pretzels, steamed hot dogs, hamburgers, peanuts and popcorn, candy and ice cream, sandwiches—the list is much too long to ever catalog.

At the end of the day, most of these pushcarts disappear, towed away behind cars or bicycles, or pushed slowly along the side of the street (probably tying up traffic) to wherever it is that pushcarts sleep. But some can be found busy all night long, providing inexpensive meals, quick snacks, or something warm to drink for the night people of the city.

They're a New York institution and the locals use them for grab-and-go meals when there isn't even time for a pastrami on pumpernickel from the deli. Try them for lunch one day for a genuine taste of New York.

finish one and, if you're in the middle of sightseeing, it's hard to take the leftovers along. You can get a sandwich just as tasty but half as large—and at a quarter of the price—at five or six other places within a hundred yards.

New York City is rich in lunch counters, diners, and small restaurants where you can get a quick lunch, and if we feel like a burger and fries, this is where we head. It's cheap, cooked to order, and comes with fries the fast food places will never top.

Restaurants Galore

Even if you eat back at the apartment most nights, you'll want to treat everybody to dinner in a nice restaurant at least once. If you're staying in a hotel, restaurant meals will be a mainstay.

If you feel like spending $150 per person on a meal in New York, don't fret: You'll have no trouble finding a place that expensive. But if, as it is for the Lains, economy is important to you, don't fret: You can eat inexpensively, even in midtown Manhattan.

In many places, local law requires restaurants to display their menus outside or in the window. That's a great convenience for patrons, who can stroll down the street looking for a place that matches their taste—and the budget. While New York restaurants are not required to post their menus, many do, especially in areas with a lot of tourist traffic.

That's ideal for families. You can make sure restaurants have something everyone will enjoy, and you can make sure you can pay for the meal when you've finished. Even areas like the theater district, which is awash in restaurants a banker can't afford, have countless cheaper alternatives.

Some of the best—and least expensive—meals you can find will be ethnic. New York City is home to members of every nation under the sun, and most of them seem to own restaurants. On vacation in an exciting, vibrant city is the perfect opportunity to experiment with things you can't get at home.

Food, New York Style

On the other hand, for foreign visitors, a taste of home can be relaxing and comforting, especially for children, in the midst of all the new sights and experiences. Either way, New York has a tempting assortment of restaurants. On my past few trips I've eaten Italian, Greek, Colombian, Peruvian, Thai, Russian, Chinese, Brazilian, Mexican, Egyptian, French, Japanese, Indian, Scandinavian, Moroccan, and a few other cuisines I can't recall. Oh—and American. And most of the ethnic restaurants cost much less than the more ordinary places nearby.

For the sorts of restaurants you'll be going to, reserving a table usually won't be necessary, especially if you eat early. Away from the theater district, restaurants often don't begin to fill up until 8 o'clock or later. Like many other big-city residents, New Yorkers tend to eat late because it takes time after work to get home, relax a bit, and go somewhere else for dinner. If you eat between 6 and 7 P.M., you'll usually have less competition for tables.

Eating out can be expensive, but it doesn't have to be. Eating out can be ordinary, with the same sorts of things you eat when you're back home, but it doesn't have to be. Wherever you go in the city, whether it's Manhattan or one of the boroughs, you'll find an exciting assortment of tastes and a price you can afford. It would be foolish not to take advantage of it.

Here's one more option, perfect for a day in the park, an afternoon at the beach, or a relaxed evening supper: Go for a picnic! Picnics don't have to be elaborate affairs with charcoal grills and a basketful of food. Stop by the local grocery store or deli and pick up sandwiches or simple food like bread, cheese, cold cuts, potato chips and the like, get some beverages (alcoholic drinks are not allowed in

Tip: *Service is seldom included in the price. Waiters and waitresses are often paid less than minimum wage and make up the rest of their income from gratuities. A tip of 15% is appropriate unless service is very poor. Tipping is not expected in fast food restaurants, deli counters, or for carry-out food.*

NYC parks), add some dessert like candy or bakery treats, put everything in a couple of plastic bags—and you have a picnic!

We've often spent all or part of a day doing just this. Sundays are favorite times because we can take some thick Sunday newspapers, a deck of cards, a ball, or other game, and a couple of bags of good things to eat, find a grassy spot under a shady tree (you get bonus points for finding one within listening distance of an afternoon band concert) and settle in for the day. It's a wonderful change of pace from the hectic rush of sightseeing and does wonders for everyone's disposition. There's plenty of space for kids to run around when they feel inclined, and plenty of time for everyone to relax, nap, read, talk, plan, or just watch clouds float past.

It doesn't always work quite as well in the winter—but we've done it on a sunny mild day! At least for a little while.

Some of our favorite meals have been picnics.

Everywhere you go in New York City, you'll be tempted by interesting-sounding restaurants, by luscious aromas escaping from windows, by artistic displays of meats, fish, or produce in neighborhood markets, by foods you've never seen or by exotic

Be sure to try a big slice of New York style pizza

variations on food you thought you knew well. You might even be driven to wonder, with some awe, where it all comes from, how they ever manage to get all this food in its mind-bending variety right to where it's needed at the precise time you happen to be hungry.

Whatever else you enjoy doing on your New York holiday, you're certain to enjoy eating.

Recommendations

✔ If you're staying in an apartment, eat breakfast and supper at "home" for maximum savings. But treat yourselves to at least one nice restaurant dinner.

✔ Don't stick to the same types of food you eat at home. This is a great time to be adventurous with an ethnic food you've never had before.

✔ Be sure to try the pizza, deli sandwiches, and bagels. New York does these better than anywhere else in the world.

✔ Don't eat at your hotel unless somebody else is paying the bill.

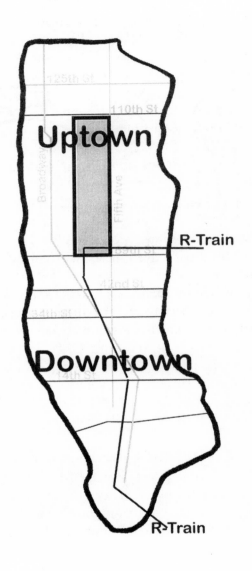

Subway Information

6. On the Go

New York City is so huge that it can be intimidating to the first-time visitor. Even tourists from Chicago, London, or Sydney are often unprepared for the magnitude of the place. New York is known as "the city that never sleeps," but to the new arrival it looks like the city that never ends.

Don't let it throw you. New York City is just as manageable as anyplace else, and part of the idea of Living Like a Local is to learn how to get around the city with the ease of a native. That's what this chapter is all about. In just a few pages, you'll be as confident in your ability to move about the city as any New Yorker.

Outfitting the Expedition

Tackling New York isn't very much like mounting a Himalayan assault, but you can follow the lead of travelers to more remote corners of the world. Preparing yourself with a few essentials will make your trip more comfortable and more convenient.

Shoes
When we travel, we often walk ten times farther—or more—than we usually do each day at home. At the very least we're on our feet more, meandering through museums, walking to the

subway station, strolling along a beach. You do *not* want to scrimp on shoes. One of the most miserable trips I ever took was one on which I did a lot of sightseeing on foot on my arrival day, wearing shoes that didn't fit quite right. I raised blisters that lasted for my entire three-week trip and I felt wretched the whole time.

Each person should bring at least two pairs of comfortable shoes. Best are shoes with good support that are well broken in. Alternate your pairs of shoes each day, or put on a different pair, with a fresh pair of socks, before you go out for the evening. Your feet will thank you for it. It's also worth bringing plastic bandages or bunion pads to put on sore spots as soon as they develop, before they've had a chance to rub into blisters.

Maps

You can find anything in New York—anything except a decent map of the city. The free tourist map of London is excellent, the one for Paris is just mediocre. But both cities are well covered by an assortment of inexpensive, comprehensive atlases. Not so New York. Maps of Manhattan abound. But tourist maps for areas outside Manhattan are almost non-existent. The assumption seems to be that *no one* would dream of going to Brooklyn! We sometimes use a city map published by the auto club we belong to, but it unfolds to about the size of a bedsheet and is in type small enough to be a problem for my no-longer-young eyes.

You can find city atlases, but some are years out of date and often don't have subways marked on the street grid. I use the *5 Borough Pocketatlas* published by the Geographica Map Company of Weehawken, NJ. Son Rik, who lives in the city, painstakingly drew in all the subway lines for me. Nice guy, Rik. The company also publishes a larger size. The new *NY@tlas* by VanDam, Inc., is also good but is more expensive and rather thick.

I sense a business opportunity here.

Daypacks

In real life most of us travel pretty light, although Barb sometimes brings a purse that couldn't be carried by an infantryman. When I travel, though, I usually find it useful to carry a daypack.

This is nothing more than a medium-sized bag for holding the accouterments you might need when you're cut off from your home base for the day. I have a lightweight nylon briefcase with a detachable shoulder strap that serves. Barb has a large purse or, sometimes, a canvas tote bag that zips closed. Kids are used to hauling around backpacks. All of these do double-duty as carry-ons for the plane or train. The keys are that the bag be lightweight and that it zips or snaps shut. You get extra credit of it has a few separate sections or compartments.

I use my daypack for carrying my camera and a few extra rolls of film, my map, an emergency snack like a granola bar or two, an umbrella if there's a chance of rain, a guidebook if I need one, a water bottle if it's warm, my journal, sunglasses and reading glasses. The daypack makes it easy for me to carry small purchases or museum guidebooks I acquire during the day. I'm seldom without it.

Safety

If you watch more television than is good for you, your mental image of New York City might be one of constant car chases, random shootings, and muggers lurking around every corner. One friend insisted that it was tacitly understood that normal people could ride the subway until 10 P.M. and after that it was inhabited only by drug addicts and crazy people.

None of that is true.

New York has become one of America's safest big cities. By the standards of other important world centers like London, Paris, Tokyo, and comparable places, it is unfortunately true that New York has more than its share of crime. But sensible tourists seldom have problems of any sort, and I won't lead you into seedy areas anywhere in this book. If New York *really* had a violence rate corresponding to what we see on television, in two years its population would shrink from 8 million to something more the size of Crown Point, Indiana!

• We take the same precautions in New York that we take when we travel anywhere—inside or outside the United States.

• Carry your wallet in a side pocket, not in the back where it's easily picked.

• Don't flash your cash.

• Keep most of your money and a spare credit card in your moneybelt or neck pouch. Carry only enough for the day in your wallet.

• Never leave your camera, purse or daypack unattended—not even for ten seconds.

• Avoid deserted areas or neighborhoods that are poorly lit after dark.

• If a place doesn't feel right to you—leave!

• Purses and daypacks should have straps that go over the shoulder.

• Pay attention to your surroundings.

These common-sense rules will produce a safer trip whether your destination is New York or Crown Point. If you take the same sensible precautions in New York that you would traveling *anywhere*, you should have no problems at all.

Getting Around

New York City is huge. From the North Bronx to Brooklyn's Coney Island is almost 25 miles (40km). From the western shore of Staten Island to northeastern Queens is more than 30 miles (50km). Driving is a needless chore. A former neighbor, on a temporary work assignment in a New York suburb, decided one Sunday afternoon to drive into the city to see the sights. Even with the relatively light Sunday traffic, it took him two hours to get to midtown Manhattan, and the traffic required such careful attention that he couldn't see anything at all from the car. When he finally got to the area near the Empire State Building, the thing he most wanted to see, he could find nowhere at all to park. Snarling, he gave up and drove back to Long Island, never having set foot outside his car.

There are better choices. Let's look at them.

Subway

New York's vast subway system is less easy to use than its counterparts in London or Washington, D.C. It's less clean and quiet than the almost antiseptic metros in Paris and Montreal. But there's not a better transportation value on Earth. You can ride anywhere—including the A train from 207th Street at the northwestern extreme of Manhattan for 31 miles to Rockaway Park Beach in southeastern corner of Queens—for just $1.50. Trains are blessedly air-conditioned in the broiling city summer.

New York's mass transit lagged behind that of other major cities for years, requiring customers to purchase individual tokens to ride the trains, while many other cities had moved on to machine-readable paper tickets good for multiple rides. That's all changed now. While you can still buy and use the old tokens for now, they're destined for oblivion.

Tip: In Manhattan, numbered Avenues run north-south and Streets run east-west. In the other boroughs that is not necessarily the case.

Paying Your Fare: You'll want to use the MetroCard instead. There are several choices, but two especially useful ones. First, you can pay for a specific number of rides. Go to the change booth and ask for a 10-ride MetroCard and you'll be charged $15. (As a bonus, you'll actually receive eleven rides for every ten you buy.) The advantage to this is that family members can share the cards.

The other good choice is to buy a pass good for unlimited rides. These can be used only by one person, but it's a terrific value and the approach I recommend. A MetroCard good for one week's worth of unlimited rides costs just $17. Because subway travel is so much a way of life for most New Yorkers (including temporary ones like you), it doesn't take long to save money. In fact, I usually buy a one-week pass even if I plan to be in the city only three or four days, knowing I'll save money over paying by the ride. If you're staying for a long time, 30 days' worth of unlimited riding costs $63. There is no fare discount for children.

MetroCards can be purchased from the change booth inside all subway stations or with a credit card from machines in major stations. The MetroCard is valid as soon as you buy it.

The card is simple to use. Just hold it with the magnetic strip facing away from you and at the bottom, slide it through the slot on the right side of the turnstile, and walk through. You will not need the card to get out of the subway again, as you do in some other cities.

Subways are easy to navigate. Really!

Using the Subway System: Get a free map (called "The Map") of the subway system for each member of your family from the change booth in any station. Each of the 468

> ***Tip:*** *Check your map. It might be faster and easier to walk a block or two and catch a direct train on another line than to take the nearest train and have to change.*

stations also has large maps of the network posted so you can plan your route. The system consists of 25 interlocking lines designated by a letter or number within a circle, and color coded. In many cities, each line has a different color. That's not the case in New York City, but generally speaking, lines with the same colors often cover similar parts of the city.

The basics of the system are simple. Note where you are and where you want to go. If they're on the same line, it's easy to get there—just ride to your station and get off. If they're on different lines, you'll have to change trains. Look for a station where the two lines intersect. Stations where you can change from one line to another are indicated with white circles or ovals on The Map.

When you go through the turnstile, you'll need to know which stairs to take down to the platform. If you're in Manhattan, *Uptown* is north toward the Bronx, and *Downtown* is south toward Battery Park. Some trains will give you their ultimate destination. The R Line, for example, runs through three boroughs. If you board that train in Manhattan, a glance at The Map will show you that a Brooklyn-bound R Train will go downtown, then cross under the river and continue south in Brooklyn. If the train is bound for Queens, it heads uptown, then turns east, goes under the river, and cuts eastbound through Queens.

Be aware, too, that some trains list their terminating station. You might want to consult your map to see that the train that's going to Coney Island is heading all the way through Brooklyn and the train for South Ferry ends at the tip of Manhattan.

It looks complicated but one day is all anyone will need to feel at home on the system. Here are a few more tips on riding the subway:

• Every subway car has a map of the entire system in it, but unlike what you expect to find in most other cities, not all cars display maps of just the route you're on. That would be a nice addition to the system.

• Some trains are *express* trains and don't stop at all stations. You can find a chart at the bottom of The Map telling you which trains are express. They're much faster, but of little use to you if they skip the station where you want to get off.

• The same set of tracks is often used by different lines. Make sure you board the right train. The line number is brightly lit on the front of every train and there's a display board next to each train door giving the line number and direction or destination of the train.

• The subway system is more than a century old and as a result, few stations are handicapped accessible. There's a list on The Map.

• The subway runs 24 hours a day, seven days a week. Very late at night it's best to wait for the train near the change booth or in designated areas in the center of the platform. They're marked with large yellow signs reading "Wait here for after hours trains." Late-night trains are usually shorter and may not extend as far down the platform as usual. And these waiting areas are closely monitored by security personnel.

• The subway runs all night, but not all station entrances are open. Station entrances displaying lighted green globes or other green lights are open 24 hours. Red globes or lights mean that entrance is closed after a certain time. A sign will direct you to the nearest open entrance, usually just across the street or at the next intersection.

• Make sure everyone can get on the train. You do *not* want to try to hold the door open: They shut with surprising—and painful!—force.

On the Go

Everyone who might be traveling alone should have his or her own copy of the subway map and knows how to use it. If you get separated, at least that way you can all get back together again. We always review the train, direction, changes, and destination stations with everyone before we board a train, so everyone know what we're doing if we get split up somehow.

Buses

It's often better and faster to hop on a bus than to take the subway. They go to more places than the subway, are a lot more scenic, and can be a godsend for sore feet and aching legs.

Your MetroCard will work on the bus just as easily as it does on the subway. Just slide it notch down into the card reader next to the driver. The card is pulled into the machine briefly, then pops back out. You can also use subway tokens or coins ($1.50) on buses. The change booth at most subway stations can provide you with bus maps of the borough you're in, although not always other boroughs. Maps are clear and easy to use, showing the route taken by every bus in the borough. Most buses stop every two or three blocks and you can use a pullcord or touchplate to signal the driver that you want to get off at the next stop.

Tip: Let the kids take turns planning your route. That way everyone will know how to use the system themselves, Mom and Dad will feel more at ease in case someone gets separated from the group, and the kids will feel safer and more independent.

Since we usually buy weekly MetroCards, good for unlimited rides, we often use buses going our way just for a brief rest from walking for a few blocks—usually late in the day when we've been on our feet for hours. If we had pay-per-ride MetroCards, however, it probably wouldn't be worth $1.50 just to save a short walk like that.

If you use a MetroCard, transfers between buses, or between

the bus and subway systems, are free within two hours.

Most buses operate only within a single borough. A few, which charge extra, operate between boroughs. The bus map will show you where to catch those, if you want, though the subway is a much better deal for going between boroughs.

Taxis

The kids (and probably you, too, if you've never seen it) will be amazed by the churning yellow river that runs through midtown Manhattan, fed by countless tributaries, sweeping everything before it... but pausing each time it reaches a stoplight. This is New York's river of taxis, impressive and irresistible as the untamed Colorado River, yellow cab after yellow cab, as far as the eye can see!

We don't take taxis very often. You can't even get into one for the price of a bus or subway ride, because there's the minimum charge of about $2 on the meter as soon as you open the door.

Taxis are usually easy to find—except late at night when they seem to turn into pumpkins

But there are times you might be willing to pay what it takes if you're toting luggage, if the weather is bad, if you're too weary to move another step, or if you or your child is hopelessly and irredeemably lost.

To hail a cab, just stand at the curb and wave at an approaching taxi. A taxi can carry four passengers, but you'll pay a small additional charge for more than two passengers or for luggage. You'll also be expected to tip the driver 10-15% of the fare.

Taxi drivers are unlikely to take you by a circuitous route to run up the bill, but you can always ask for an estimated fare before you get in. The basic charge from LaGuardia or Kennedy airports to Midtown will be about $30. You should be able to go anywhere in Manhattan for less than that, unless you're going a long way at the peak of rush hour.

Taxis can take you anywhere in Manhattan with ease, but drivers' knowledge of other boroughs is uneven. Tell the driver where you want to go before you get into the cab and make sure he (It will almost always be a "he") knows where it is. Driving a cab is often one of the first jobs newcomers in the city get and it's not uncommon to encounter a driver whose command of English or of the geography of the city beyond Manhattan is at least inexact. But we've always gotten where we're going, and at a fair price. Remind me to tell you my Brooklyn taxi story later.

Outside of Manhattan it can be difficult to hail a taxi in the street. The locals often call car services. There's one—often several—in every neighborhood, listed in the Yellow Pages. When you call, tell them where you want to go and they'll quote you a price. Confirm the fare with your driver when he picks you up. Prices will be comparable to a regular taxi.

Ferries

One mode of transport everyone will want to ride is the ferry. Best value is the Staten Island Ferry from Battery Park, at the southern tip of Manhattan, across to Staten Island. There are several attractions on the island that we'll talk about later, but even if you just ride over and come straight back, everyone will enjoy the trip, and the picture-book view of the downtown skyline.

It's similar to the view you get riding the ferry out to the Statue of Liberty and Ellis Island with one difference: The Staten Island Ferry is free!

If you'd like to pay for a more extensive and spectacular cruise, several companies including Circle Line and NY Waterway offer several trips per day, from one to three hours long, that cover just some of the sights or go all the way around Manhattan. You can also take a ferry to games at the baseball stadiums. Websites are listed at the end of the book.

On Foot

This is our favorite mode of transportation. Our kids claimed that was because it's free, but that's only part of the attraction. Walking lets you get the real feel of a place, gives you a chance to turn aside and strike off in a direction you hadn't planned, provides the constant opportunity to be surprised and delighted by the small things bus and subway travelers zip right past… or right beneath… and never imagine are there.

When you walk, you see how the pieces of a place fit together. Sights are connected, they aren't just stand alone images. A city is populated by real people, not just subway cashiers and museum guards. Walking lets you slow down and savor the city, gives you more to remember and reflect on, instead of leaving you with fragmented images of too many sights in too little time.

Let's start walking with a Family Travel series tradition—the first day walking tour of the city's highlights:

The Lain Walking Tour of Midtown Manhattan

Writing a book about a place as large and complex as New York City presents a lot of problems but the chief one is this: *There's so much to choose from. How do I pick?* Where shall we go for our orientation walk? Do we walk along the Hudson River and with the Statue of Liberty on our left and the slender twin towers of the World Trade Center on our right? Saunter across the Brooklyn Bridge and make our way to colorful Chinatown? Wander down Museum Mile alongside Central Park?

No. Those are all good choices worth doing, and I'm going to nag you to do them all before you leave town. But you want a first-day walk in New York City that has as much of the flash and glamour of the place as you can find. So let me take you on a two-hour stroll through the heart of Manhattan, where the kids can see so many of the sights they've experienced only in books and movies before today.

We'll walk about four miles at an easy pace, but you can devote either more or less time to the walk by turning aside when you see something that looks interesting or a place you want to visit right away, or by cutting the walk short if you get tired and hopping on one of the many subways or buses that are just steps away. Sound good? Then tighten the laces on your shoes and follow me!

Central Park South: A great place to begin our walk is at Grand Army Plaza, the corner of Fifth Avenue and Central Park South on the N and R lines of the subway. It's a busy and fun place. If the weather is nice you can watch local artists painting in the plaza. Lined up along the curb are horses and carriages, waiting for customers who want a romantic ride through Central Park. I don't think I've ever been romantic enough to pay $30 or more for a 20 minute ride... but that's just me. At least petting the horses is free. Across the street is the Plaza Hotel, one of the most famous hotels in the world.

After we pet a horse, we're going to stroll west along the street and look into Central Park. We'll come back here in Chapter 16 and spend a whole day. For now, though, we'll walk

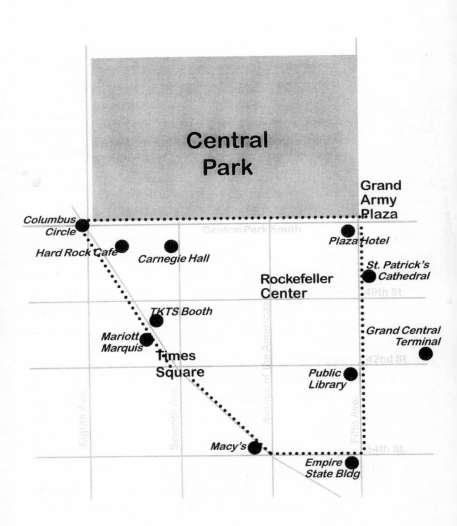

The Lain Walk

along the fence and look through the trees at the picturesque *Pond*, so serene that it seems out of place in the middle of a city of 8 million people. As you walk, the quiet of the park on your right contrasts with the traffic on your left. Many of the buildings across the street are hotels, and a room overlooking the park can be dazzlingly expensive. Right now, you have the same view for free.

When you come to the end of the park, you're at *Columbus Circle*. The skyscraper across the street is the Trump International Hotel and Tower, built by one of the city's wealthiest modern developers, Donald Trump. We hope you're not finished walking yet, but subways A, B, C, D, 1, and 9 stop here, along with M-buses 5, 7, 10, 20, and 104. Busy place!

But don't quit yet. The walk gets even more exciting. Cross the street and go clockwise around the circle to the first left, just a short distance. Now you're on *Broadway*, and if there's a more famous street in the world, I've never heard of it. The first time I was here, I stood on the sidewalk and quietly sang "Happy Birthday" to myself, just so I could go home and tell friends that I once sang on Broadway. Feel free to do that... if you want to look for new friends.

Let's walk down this busy street. Stay on the left side, but if you want to cross it for any reason, please do it only at a stoplight. There's not a busier street in America and I hate it when my readers get run down in the street, as you will if you cross in the middle of the block. New York drivers are not famous for their patience.

If you're hungry for a touristy lunch, you can turn left at 57th Street. The entrance to the *Hard Rock Café* is just down the left side of the street. If you want to continue for another block down 57th, you'll come to *Carnegie Hall*.

Otherwise, go straight ahead. This is the *Theater District*, the "Great White Way." It's a fun walk during the day, but spectacular after dark, with more neon lights than you've ever seen. In fact, where most cities limit the size and lighting of outdoor signs, New York City has *minimum* requirements for this area.

As you stroll you'll pass theaters that are home to shows you've always wanted to see, starring actors and actresses who are household names around the world. Somebody in your group is sure to say "Let's go to a show!" Check at the box office for prices. And gasp! You can easily pay $100 or more per ticket for a Broadway show. But hang on. A solution is coming up in a couple of blocks.

As you cross 49th Street, you're in the famous *Times Square* area, although the square itself is really further down at 42nd Street. A million people pack these streets every New Year's Eve to celebrate the night, but the jostling crowds, frantic traffic, sidewalk vendors, food stands, colorful animated signs, bright theater marquees, corner musicians, and all the frenzy make this area seem like a giant street party every day of the year. This is the New York you came to see.

Look at the signs enticing you to see *Beauty and the Beast* or *Les Misérables*. Urging you to eat pizza or steaks or barbecue. Listen to the reggae band, playing for tips. You've never been to a more vibrant place. Window shop at countless electronics stores or

> *Tip:* Keep your valuables secured. There are plenty of police in the area, but also plenty of pickpockets..

sidewalk tables offering goods cheap—and cheap goods. There are still a couple of adult theaters in the area, too, tolerated mostly because tourists expect to see them. But Times Square's seedy, sleazy days are behind it, and it's a real hub of family fun now.

When you get to Duffy Square at 47th and Broadway, you'll spot a long line snaking its way up to a small booth. This is the *TKTS Booth*, where, if you're really serious about seeing a show, you can by tickets for tonight for 25 to 50 percent off the regular price. Just check the board in front to see what they have tickets for, and hope they're still available when you get to the front of the line. Cash only and tickets for today only. But you get good seats at the best available prices.

At 46th Street is the Marriott Marquis hotel. Even if you can't afford to stay there, it's worth going up to the eighth-floor lobby to gaze up at the spectacular atrium that reaches all the way up to the 46th floor, glass elevators zipping up and down a central core. The kids will insist on a ride to the top. *Some* members of our group much prefer just to wait in the lobby while others take their skyride.

Continue your walk down Broadway, soaking up the atmosphere. If you're worn out when you get to 42nd Street, you'll find fifteen different subway lines and eight bus routes within a block of the corner.

Do keep going, though, enjoying the bustle. The north-south blocks are short and pass quickly as you gawk. And as you walk, one of the most famous structures will loom above you. In ten minutes or so you'll be at 34th Street.

You never know what you'll see as you walk through the streets

Here's New York's most famous shopping haven, *Macy's*. I'm betting that someone in your group will want to go in, just to browse. And an hour later someone else will have to go in to retrieve the browser.

And that looming building we saw as we walked? The *Empire State Building*, of course. If it's a nice day or clear night, this might be a good place to interrupt our walk and go to the top for a spectacular view. Unless you can climb up the outside like King Kong, you'll have to go inside to the elevator. It's easy to find: Just get in the long line. You'll also find an assortment of subway lines and bus routes at 34th and Broadway.

We're finished with Broadway for now, because the Empire State Building is also on *Fifth Avenue*. Turn left and walk back north now. This is a great shopping street, one of the best in the world. You can spend a lot of money on Fifth Avenue, although window shopping is just as much fun.

In just a few blocks, at 41st Street, is the *New York Public Library*, one of the country's foremost temples of learning and a fun place to visit for the exhibitions. Bryant Park behind the library is a popular place for lunchers, and for free movies on summer evenings. Go back up to 42nd Street and walk a block to the right and you get to *Grand Central Station*. We'll find lots of places to shop and eat here, but we must go to its massive waiting room with the spectacular ceiling depicting the stars of the cosmos. It's an architectural marvel.

Back on Fifth Avenue, we'll continue window shopping our way northward until we reach 49th Street, where we'll take another diversion to *Rockefeller Center*, home of Radio City Music Hall (entrance on Sixth Avenue) and NBC television (on 49th). Behind the tall GE Building is the flag-bedecked *Rockefeller Plaza*. If you're visiting from late autumn to early spring, join the ice skaters on the rink below. If you didn't bring your skates, don't worry. You can rent them here.

Not much further to go now. We can go back to Fifth Avenue and shop at *Saks 5th Avenue*, then cross 50th Street and rest for a few minutes in the grandeur and serenity of *St. Patrick's Cathedral*, America's most famous Roman Catholic church.

Refreshed, we can finish shopping our way up the street until we're back at 59th Street—also known as Central Park South, our starting point. Come to think of it, maybe we *can't* do this walk in just two hours. There are far too many distractions. But that's exactly what we came for!

Recommendations

✔ A good map or atlas will make your life easier.

✔ The MetroCard is a great investment. Public transportation costs a fraction of what taxis do.

✔ Walk as much as you can. You'll see more, have more fun, and get a real feel for the city.

Historic Grand Central Terminal is a feast for the eyes

7. Cashing In

You'll need money in New York. I nearly added "—lots of money" because New York can be terribly expensive. But I didn't, because it's possible to be frugal in New York... as many of its 8 million residents prove. Whether you're spending a little or a lot, however, managing your money effectively is critical to a good holiday. Fortunately, you have a lot of choices when it comes to managing your vacation budget.

If you're coming from outside the United States, you will need American money exclusively. No one will take euros, yen, or even Canadian dollars in payment for anything. Don't worry: If there's one thing New York is good at, it's making it easy for visitors to spend money. The next section will tell you all you need to know about money—except, perhaps, how to earn it in the first place.

Four Types of Money

What's this? I just said you could use only U.S. dollars and now I say there are four types of money? Yes—four ways of acquiring and spending the dollars that New Yorkers want to extract from you. Most likely you'll use a mixture of two or three, and when the Lains travel, we use all four.

Cash

This is everybody's favorite and the easiest way to spend: Just whip out the money and that's all there is to the transaction. Sometimes that's your only choice. Taxis often take nothing but cash. Vendors selling food or newspapers from sidewalk stands take nothing but cash. Some small shops and restaurants take nothing but cash. Credit card transactions in small groceries, delis, or fast food places are sometimes difficult and time consuming, even when they're possible.

But you do *not* want to ramble around New York City with your entire vacation budget in cash—that's a disaster waiting to happen! Carry in your wallet only as much cash as you need for the day; everything else should be in one of the other forms of money below. Extra cash should be in a money belt, and we'll talk about that in a few pages, too.

If you're coming from outside the United States, cash can be a bit of a problem at first. Should you get money converted into U.S. dollars at home or bring your own currency and buy dollars in New York? In general, it's usually best to bring your money in dollars. You will need to spend money right away when you arrive for transportation to your apartment or hotel, and you'll

ATMS are everywhere for some quick cash

need American money for that. While there are currency exchanges in the airports, the rates are almost the worst you can find. You'll do better to have currency exchanged for dollars at home.

Once you're in Manhattan you will see few currency exchanges, but if you need to, you can change currencies at many banks. Outside Manhattan, currency exchange is much more difficult. But there's really no advantage to bringing your own country's currency on the trip. Bring enough cash in U.S. dollars for a day or two, and use the other three sorts of money.

If you're arriving from somewhere else in the United States, it's *still* not a good idea to carry your entire budget in cash. Too many bad things can happen. The advice is the same: Have enough money for a couple of days at most, and read the rest of the chapter.

Credit Cards

Credit cards are a great convenience and a great danger. They are widely accepted and eliminate the need to carry large amounts of cash. If a credit card is lost or stolen it can be cancelled and replaced with just a phone call, while lost cash will be buying somebody else's dinner tonight. What's not to like?

Well, as I said earlier, you can't use them everywhere, especially for small purchases. You may very well inspire some of that mostly mythical New York rudeness if you try to buy a 50-cent newspaper with your Visa card.

A bigger problem is that you need to keep very careful track of your spending. Most of us at some time have gotten ourselves into a hole a little deeper than we'd planned because credit cards are so easy to use. It's an even more-

Tip: *Don't use credit cards for cash advances except in the most serious emergencies. Those advances are really high-interest loans, with interest rates typically of 18–21% or more.*

dangerous trap on vacation because everything is different, there are so many exciting things to do, eat, or buy, and the debts can be racked up to formidable levels before we realize it.

Worse yet, unless you're the sort of person who pays off the bill in its entirety each month, using a credit card means that things cost more than you initially paid for them because of the interest added each month to the credit card bill. Don't pay the full amount by the end of the month and that $100 family dinner might become $102. That doesn't sound like much, but it adds up, sometimes by hundreds of dollars over a brief period of time.

Don't leave your credit cards at home, but do keep track of your spending just as carefully as you would with cash.

Debit and ATM Cards
Whether it's inside or outside our own country, this has become one of the Lains' favorite methods of paying for travel.

A debit card looks like a credit card, but when you use it, the money is deducted immediately from your account back home, so there's no bill to pay and no interest to accrue. Moreover, use it in a bank (ATM) machine and you can get quick cash in the local currency immediately. So when we travel nowadays, we carry a minimum of cash—just enough for a day or two—and withdraw more as we need it, the same way we do at home.

You'll find bank machines everywhere. They may be the only thing that's more common in New York than taxis and bagels. Sometimes they'll be behind a locked door that only a bank's customers can get through, and this can be a worry when you're out of cash and the banks are closed. But you should have little trouble in most places finding a machine you can get to.

Just remember these points. First, make sure you have enough money in your account at home to cover your use of the card. If you drain the account, the card won't work any more. Second, some banks impose a fee for each transaction, especially a withdrawal from a machine that's owned by another bank.

This can add to your costs. Check with your bank before you go. Third, remember that there is usually a limit—often $200 or $300 a day—to the amount of money you can withdraw in cash, even if you have plenty in your account. Know what your limit is so you don't get caught short.

Traveler's Checks

We used to take most of our money in traveler's checks on every vacation. We still take part of our budget that way, but not the way we did before ATMs. We like the convenience traveler's checks provide because we take money from our account before we leave and we know just what we've spent—the advantages of cash and no credit card bills to face later. The best thing about them, though, is that even if they are lost or stolen, traveler's checks can be replaced almost at once.

In the United States, traveler's checks can be used to pay stores and restaurants directly, something that is often not true in other countries where they normally have to be converted into cash in the local currency. But even in the United States, some places prefer not to take them. We don't use this form of money for domestic travel the way we did before ATMs were common, but if your credit card has already developed a twitch and you don't like drawing down your bank balance through ATMs, this is a whole lot better choice than carrying a bunch of cash.

> ***Tip:*** *If you're a member of an American auto club like AAA or a credit union, you can often get traveler's checks with no service fee. Most banks charge 1 to 2 percent of the amount purchased.*

If you're coming from outside the United States, make sure you get traveler's checks in U.S. dollars or you might have to pay two commissions—one for cashing the check and one for converting your currency to dollars. That's not a very good deal.

How Much Money Will We Need?

I *always* get asked that question when I do talks or book signings and I always struggle with it. I could probably give you a more accurate answer if you asked me what the final score will be of the next Super Bowl or World Cup final. You have to look at your own family's expectations and desires.

However, Chapter 21 should help you come up with a very realistic budget for your trip. But you won't be taking all that money in cash!

The only cash you'll need is enough to get you through the first day or two. After that, you can get more as you need it by cashing traveler's checks or visiting the bank machine. Probably you won't need to carry more than $200 or $300 divided between Mom and Dad when you arrive in the city, unless you expect to have unusual expenses.

The best approach is to use a mix of money: A few hundred dollars in cash to start, replenished as needed by visiting the bank machine or cashing some traveler's checks, with major expenses paid with a debit or credit card. Sounds like a well-balanced financial diet.

Financial Security

A section with a name like that makes it look like I'm about to try to sell you life insurance or mutual funds. But I don't want any of your money; I just want you to keep what you have.

Parents are used to planning for emergencies. We try to look ahead at what *might* happen, however unlikely, and think about how to protect our families. (Which explains why some people *do* want to sell you insurance and stocks.) Well, unfortunately, sometimes unpleasant things happen. There is always a small chance, for example, that you could lose your wallet.

It could slip out of your pocket in a restaurant or you could accidentally leave it on the counter next to the cash register in a store. Both of these have happened to me (without, fortunately,

---

Coin of the Realm

If you're visiting New York from outside the United States, you'll need American money. Your credit cards will work fine here, but when dealing in cash, only U.S. money will do. Here's a quick guide to the money system.

Paper money (called "bills" in the U.S., rather than the more common term "notes" elsewhere) is all the same size and color, regardless of value. Bills come in denominations of $1, $2, $5, $10, $20, $50, and $100, although the $2 bill is very rare. The United States introduced a revised currency design a few years ago incorporating anti-counterfeiting devices and larger portraits on the front, but you might still find a few older bills in circulation.

Coinage, at 100 cents to the dollar, most often comes in denominations of 1 cent, (written 1¢)—a copper-colored coin called a penny, and in silver-colored coins of 5, 10, and 25 cents, called a nickel, dime, and quarter respectively. The dime (10¢) is the smallest of the three, the quarter (25¢) the largest. There is also a very large, silver-colored 50¢ coin, but it is very rare.

The U.S. Mint has tried for many years to introduce a $1 coin, and a new one is now in circulation. It's about the same size as a 25¢ piece but copper-colored. Despite an enormous effort by the government to introduce the coin, it's still uncommon and probably doomed to remain so unless the government withdraws $1 bills from circulation.

any bad consequences). It's even possible—although highly unlikely, despite what the TV shows imply—that your pocket could be picked or that you could be robbed. There's an easy way to protect yourself. Do what experienced travelers to: Invest in a money belt. A money belt is just a nylon pouch that fits around your waist, under your trousers or skirt. That's where you put extra money, traveler's checks, and a spare credit card. It's invisible, comfortable, and safe. Keep all the cash you need for the day in your wallet where you can get to it, and put the rest in your money belt. If an unexpected expense requires more cash than you have on hand, a quick trip to the men's (or ladies') room allows you to retrieve extra money quickly from your belt. Some people prefer a neck pouch that goes under their shirt or blouse.

It's always a bad idea to leave cash in your hotel room or apartment, although more hotels are fitting their rooms with individual safes. But nothing is safer than dividing the family treasury between Mom and Dad, with the emergency money safely hidden beneath their clothing.

Kids and Money

The kids in the family, especially the older ones, will want money, too. Give them a fixed amount and let them be responsible for it themselves. You might give them their allotment all at once or, if they are very young or you're staying for a long visit, part of it every week.

Let them spend their money however they wish. Some of the things they buy might strike parents as trivial or juvenile. That's okay. This is a trip for them, too… and they *are* juveniles! A trinket that's meaningless to a parent might be a child's most treasured keepsake from the trip.

Unless they ask you to hold it for them, expect the kids to take care of their own money just as parents take care of the family finances. Expect them to budget their allotment. If you give each one $50 to spend on souvenirs, make sure they understand that anything beyond that must come from their own resources. A trip like this is educational on *many* levels, and this is one of them.

Recommendations

✔ Use a mix of money types: cash, credit and debit cards, and traveler's checks.

✔ Don't carry more cash than you expect to spend in one day.

✔ Buy and use a money belt or neck pouch for extra money and a spare credit card.

✔ Let the kids have some money and don't interfere in how they spend it.

8. Living Like a Local

D on't be a tourist. Okay, wait—be a tourist. You can't help
yourself. You *are* a tourist. But what I mean is, don't be
a *typical* tourist, going from attraction to attraction like
you're in some vast urban theme park where there's no
connection among the exhibits, and where the cab drivers and
waitresses and museum guards and theater ushers are only
costumed interpreters placed there for your amusement.

I've heard from a large number of readers of my other family
travel books, and if I know *anything* about the people who have
bought other books in this series, it's that they are not the sort
of folks to have an attitude like that. The reason for a family trip
like this, undertaken at considerable cost and inconvenience, is
really twofold.

First, you want to make family memories that will last forever,
that will still be talked about whenever you get together after the
kids are grown and have families of their own. Believe me—when
that happens you won't be willing to trade that conversation for
ten times what the trip cost you, plus compound interest!

The other reason to take a trip like this, to really get to know
one of the world's great cities, is so that your children can grow,
can see an important and fascinating part of their world and feel
connected to it. If you're coming to New York City from abroad,

the kids will learn that Americans are pretty much like them with the same interests and joys and fears, but that there are fascinating differences. If you're coming from somewhere else in the United States, the kids will learn the same things about New Yorkers—they're the same as Montanans, Floridians, or Wisconsinites... but with a twist.

It's why each book in this series urges you to find an apartment to live in, rather than a hotel, if you can. It's cheaper, because the per person/per day cost is usually lower and because you can fix some of your own meals. It's more comfortable because it's more than just a single room and it feels like home, not like an institution. And it's because staying in an apartment lets you become more a part of the city you're in, living exactly the same way its full-time residents live.

It's called Living Like a Local.

When you're Living Like a Local, you take a step away from the tourist world of hotels with ornate lobbies and gift shops. Your apartment will be similar to the ones in which a million New Yorkers are sleeping tonight. You'll shop for groceries at the same corner market as everyone else on your street, walk out after dark to the same neighborhood ice cream shop the nearby kids and their parents frequent, buy your *Times* and fresh bagels from the same next-door bakery each morning, and by the third day be chatting with the owner like a regular.

When you're Living Like a Local you'll still go to the same museums and parks as regular tourists, but they'll feel more like *your* museums and parks. You'll have more of a sense of the neighborhoods and communities that make up the city (regular tourists are apt to miss that entirely). You'll understand more about how *this* museum came to be here, and why *that* park is important other than as a place to walk dogs.

When you're Living Like a Local, you feel a sense of ownership of the city, a stake in it, that hotel guests never suspect is possible. And this is a key factor in your children's *really* learning about a place: Their place in the world needn't be limited to just the few square miles surrounding the bed they normally sleep in. The possibilities are far greater than just Plymouth, Indiana, or Plymouth, England. They can go, and grow, and thrive *anywhere*! If you are Living Like a Local—you become one!

A week or two in the city isn't going to make you indistinguishable from a lifelong New Yorker. But it will show the kids, and remind their parents, that we're all people of the same world, and that's a good thing to know.

So what do you need to know to become, if only for a little while, a Local?

The Weather

You don't let the weather dictate what you do at home, do you? ("Sorry, Boss. I won't be coming to work today. It's raining and a bit chilly....") Then don't let weather interfere with your vacation plans, either. Heat, snow, rain—we've enjoyed ourselves in all of them in New York.

In fact, the city *is* subject to extremes. In the summer you might occasionally encounter days of 100 degrees Fahrenheit (38C). That's why I told you to ask about air-conditioning in the apartments in Chapter 2. In the winter the temperature can drop to 0F (-18C) with a foot (.3m) of snow. Neither is likely, but they're both possible. Typical weather, if there's any such thing in New York, might be:

	DAYTIME	NIGHTTIME
Winter	25 to 45F	15 to 35F
	-4 to 7C	-9 to 2C
Spring and Autumn	50 to 70F	40 to 55F
	10 to 21C	4 to 13C
Summer	75 to 95F	55 to 75F
	24 to 35C	13 to 24C

Spring and late autumn can be damp, but all-day rains are uncommon. Summers are usually dry, but you can encounter the odd shower. It doesn't snow a lot in New York, but when it does, it is often with some enthusiasm.

If that weather forecast sounds pretty broad, it is. New York gets a bit of everything. Remember, too, that the city is very large and it's perfectly likely that while there might be a thunderstorm over Central Park that would do credit to a rainforest, the sun might be shining in Brooklyn's Prospect Park. I've always thought that leaving the subway was an adventure because the weather was sure to be different from where I got on—I just didn't know whether it would be better or worse.

The final word on weather: If you let it affect your trip, better stay home. There's weather everywhere.

Media

It's always hard to keep up with the outside world while we're on a trip. Come to think of it, maybe that's one reason we like to travel. A lot goes on in the world we might not *want* to know about.

But if you *do* want to know what's going on, New York City is a good place to find out.

Print Media

Three major daily papers are published in New York City: the *New York Times*, perhaps the best of America's 1,700 daily papers, and the tabloid-size *Post* and *Daily News*. The Long Island daily *Newsday* circulates widely in the city, and the financial paper *The Wall Street Journal* is published here five days a week.

But there are many more choices. News vendors and shops in Manhattan carry Sunday newspapers from all over the United States, and dailies from many eastern cities. Daily papers from some European capitals and Sunday editions from all over the world are easy to find, especially in the area around Times Square.

The foreign language press thrives in New York City as it does nowhere else because of the many languages spoken in the city. Newspapers are published here daily or weekly in Arabic, Chinese, Hebrew, Russian, Spanish, and other languages, and are available in central Manhattan. Away from Midtown, foreign language publications abound in ethnic neighborhoods. You can find a good selection of Russian language publications in Brighton Beach, tons of Chinese publications in Chinatown, Spanish publications of all sorts in East Harlem and the Upper East Side, and so on.

Broadcast Media

The area is served by more than a dozen terrestrial television stations, although reception can be spotty because the many tall buildings can interfere with the signals. That's why many apartments and most hotels offer cable television with 50 or more channels of entertainment.

The radio scene is even more diverse, with dozens of stations offering every type of programming and broadcasting in Spanish, Polish, Korean, and many other languages besides English.

Laundry

You'll have no problem finding a self-service laundry in any residential area of the city, but expect to pay up to $2 a load to wash. But if you're staying for two or three weeks, clean clothes are a luxury without price after everything's been worn several times!

Health

Nowhere in the world has more complete medical facilities. If the worst happens, it couldn't happen in a better place.

In an emergency, telephone 911.

If you're coming from somewhere else in the United States, your own health insurer will probably cover any emergency care you need, but details vary. Emergency facilities are available at hospitals in every neighborhood of the city.

If you're coming from abroad, be aware that the United States is one of the few nations on Earth without a national health program. Hospital emergency departments will usually treat visitors with life-threatening conditions without charge, but payment for other care normally will have to be arranged in advance through a credit card or evidence of insurance.

Appropriate Attire

I beg your pardon? I don't understand the question.

There's no dress code in New York, except in a few restaurants and nightclubs. But New Yorkers are a diverse and open-minded bunch and you'll be welcomed anywhere in clothes that are clean and not in tatters. (In unclean, tattered clothes, you might be tolerated—but not necessarily welcomed.) Two women even won a lawsuit a few years ago permitting them to ride the subway topless, although I've never actually seen anyone do that.

Whatever you wear at home will be just fine in New York. Bring casual, seasonal clothing. If you want to dress a little sharper to go to nice restaurants or to a Broadway show, that's a good place for it.

New York Attitude: What's It to Ya?

If you've read *Paris for Families*, you'll recall that much of the early discussion in this chapter was devoted to debunking the "Rude Parisian" myth. The reputation of New Yorkers for being rude to visitors is probably even more fearsome.

And no more true.

Like big-city people everywhere, New Yorkers can be brusque and loud. And I believe they take a certain pride in their reputation for rude indifference. But the indifference is just for show. Almost everyone will go out of their way to help you.

Remember the taxi story I promised you? Here it is. Barb and I arrived at LaGuardia late one night and got in a taxi. We asked the driver to take us to the Brooklyn Marriott, a brand-new hotel in downtown Brooklyn, open just a few weeks. Problem 1: Our taxi driver didn't know where it was and we didn't have the street address. Even the registration confirmation slip from the hotel just said "Downtown Brooklyn." Problem 2: Our Chinese taxi driver understood very little English and spoke less. We finally got across the idea that he should just go to downtown Brooklyn and drive around the main streets. We'd be sure to spot it, we assumed.

We drove the streets of downtown Brooklyn for fifteen minutes, our driver coming ever closer to panic, shouting "Where? Where? No hotel!" (Aside: It was a performance better than almost any Broadway show I've seen.)

Finally at a stop light he rolled down his window and screamed at the driver next to us, "Where Marriott?"

Almost any attire is acceptable *in New York*

The other driver, a distinguished-looking middle-aged Arab, couldn't understand the heavily Chinese-accented English and shouted questions. The Chinese driver couldn't understand the Arabic-accented English and we sat at the light through a full cycle while the men shouted at each other uncomprehendingly.

Finally I (who was able to make out both versions of English) began to translate, like some United Nations linguist. And in this way, the Arab driver was able to direct the Chinese driver to the hotel, six blocks away.

The story didn't end there, and this is the real point: The Arab driver wanted to make sure we understood correctly, so he followed us to the hotel, watched us get safely out of the cab, waved, made a U-turn in the middle of the street, and went back to his business.

Typical New York: Lots of shouting and arm waving, with real kindness underneath.

Things like this happen to me all the time. I was looking for an obscure museum one afternoon and was stopped three times by people who saw me studying my map, notebook, and building signs. All wanted to help. The first was a young black construction worker, who directed me down the proper side street. The second was an old Jewish lady who pointed me to the right building. The third was a middle-aged Italian man, who told me why the museum had closed temporarily and where some of its exhibits could now be found.

I didn't ask any of them—they saw a lost soul and tried to save it.

A friend recently wrote to me about her own encounter on a Christmastime shopping expedition to Macy's:

> I was at the jewelry counter purchasing some earrings for my sister. The clerk was an attractive young woman... working very efficiently... with seemingly no interest in idle conversation. After she had taken my money and given me my purchase, I reached over and touched her hand, saying, "Thank you. I hope you have a wonderful Christmas season." Her eyes filled with tears... and she

responded with "Thank you... you've made my day..." I'll never forget that moment. Such a simple thing. No matter where you are, people appreciate kindness.

That's New York. Arab, Chinese, Italian, Jewish, black, white, young, old—the total human package. Don't be put off by the brashness, the loudness, the aloofness. I love New Yorkers. But don't tell them I said so: they'd pretend not to like it.

Recommendations

✔ As much as you can, Live Like a Local, not a tourist. You'll learn more, enjoy more, appreciate more.

✔ Enjoy the incredible diversity of people in New York. It's a microcosm of the world and the more people you talk to, the more fun you'll have—and the more about people your kids will learn. Give people a chance to be helpful. They'll enjoy it, and so will you.

For the latest updates to *New York City for Families*, check out our page on the web at:

www.interlinkbooks.com/nycforfamilies.html

Part II
N.Y. Adventures

If you're still with me at this point, you must be convinced: New York is a place we've got to visit! Excellent! Now you've got more questions, all revolving around the idea *What should we see and do while we're there?* That's the question I'll be answering in Part II. Chapter 9 will tell you just how to use the rest of this book, and in Chapters 10 to 18 we'll check out more than 180 family-friendly museums, walks, parks, activities, and surprises your family can experience. Obviously that doesn't cover every possibility that New York offers, but here is the very cream—the best that New York has for families.

You can't possibly do it all and if you try, you'll put yourself in the hospital. I'll show you how to pick and choose among the activities and how to get the most out of your time in the city. This section will take you to the famous places like the Statue of Liberty and the Empire State Building, of course, but they will also lead you to places you never knew existed that might be the highlight of the trip for one of your group. As you plan the details of your itinerary, these are chapters to read and discuss together—the very heart of your trip!

9. How Do We Choose?

The chapters in the first part of the book were organizational—traveling, eating, finding someplace to sleep. But now we're faced with the most intimidating task in the book: How, among all the thousands of things to see and do in New York, do we choose?

Let's get one thing straight—You just can't do everything.

There are a few larger cities on earth, but none is more varied, more complex, more filled with possibilities. The only way to "do it all" is to live to be a thousand years old, and to dedicate every day of your life to it.

So *New York City for Families* doesn't cover everything. The chapters that follow will lay out a broad range of family-friendly activities that is sure to include favorites for every member of your entourage, but even choosing from among a hundred or so carefully selected activities can be daunting. This chapter will help.

Planning Is Important… and So Is Spontaneity

Careful planning is the key to a successful family vacation. When you're hauling an entire group hundreds or thousands of miles to a place as jam-packed with activities and people as New York City, you dare not show up with no plan in mind; you'll see three or four famous things that everybody else sees, but you'll miss equally wonderful things that are right next door. Without planning, your vacation will cost you much more than necessary and you'll get less value for your money. Without planning, you'll never know all the neat things you might have done... until your better-organized neighbors come back from *their* trip to New York with memories and photographs galore!

At the same time, over-planning is absolutely deadly. Nothing will make the kids (or their parents) more surly than marching relentlessly from one museum to another, doing everything by the clock and feeling crushed under a self-imposed obligation to check off, one-by-one, every item on a massive sightseeing list. If I wanted my family to have *that* kind of fun, we'd just join the army!

The chapters that follow describe the very best that New York City has to offer the kids in your family. Everybody should read them, if they're old enough, because they'll provide ideas nobody would have thought of.

Next, go to the Planning Pages in Part III. Chapter 19 provides a complete list of all the attractions featured in the book, and is perfect to use for everyone to vote for their favorites. Finally, Chapter 20 shows you how to take all those ideas and put together a great itinerary.

Just one more point, though: One of our favorite parts of traveling together was leaving ourselves room to be surprised, to suddenly toss our list aside and do something else. Maybe we wanted to spend extra time at a place we found fascinating. Maybe an attraction wasn't as much fun as we'd expected. Maybe we spotted something not on our list at all and went to investigate.

That's great! Do it! Of course you'll have a list of things to do when you get to the city. But just maybe you'll discover something else that's even better. Are there jugglers performing on the sidewalk in Times Square? Stop and watch them! Do you see a motorcade pulling up in front of St. Patrick's Cathedral?

Unless you're planning to move to New York, there is much more to see and do in the next nine chapters than any sane person would want to attempt. But those chapters, describing the very best family-friendly attractions in the city, will provide all you need for a phenomenal family trip.

All the information was accurate when this book went to press, but things will change, and no one is likely to ask my permission beforehand. One reason listings do not include exact admission prices or opening hours is because those are the things that change most often. Many museums close one day per week, often Mondays. This information is included. Check the Web page for this book before your trip for updated information. The page is at:

www.interlinkbooks.com/nycforfamilies.

There is also an e-mail link on that page for you to contact me with any needed updates you discover on your trip.

Attractions in the chapters that follow are listed like this:

Empire State Building [Fifth Ave. at 34th St., Midtown. Subway B, D, F, N, Q, R, and W: 34th St. Observation deck usually open until midnight].

In brackets after the name of the attraction (or at the end of a lengthy entry) is its address or location. Next is the borough where you can find the attraction, or the area of Manhattan it's in. That is followed by the nearest subway lines and the stations they serve. After that the entry lists days the attraction is closed,

Hang around until you see what dignitary is visiting the Cardinal of New York.

You should arrive with a plan. But it's only a plan, not a contract. New York has more surprises than a magician. Let New York work its magic on you.

Three Rules of Family Travel

You can be certain that a family trip like this one will be something everyone will remember for the rest of their lives. Whether they remember it with joy or with horror—that's another matter! Here is the very best advice the Lain family can offer, the three keys to keeping everybody cheerful, cooperative, and congenial traveling companions.

1. Everybody gets their first choice

When we went to a new place, we always put together a list of attractions, like the one in Chapter 19. We talked about everything, and asked the kids to rank them as Must-See, Maybe, or No Way! Finally we asked them to *or unusual hours of operation. Unless specified otherwise, most attractions open between 9 and 10 A.M. and close between 4 and 6 P.M. Hours may be longer in the summer and shorter in the winter. Unfortunately these things change faster than any printing press can keep up with, so only hours that vary significantly from the norm are specified. Finally, free attractions are specified, or the age under which admission is free.*

mark the one thing they would be most disappointed to miss.

Frankly, sometimes the No. 1 thing on somebody's list was something no one else was interested in at all... especially Mom and Dad. But these trips were for the *family*. Barb and I knew we'd have a chance to travel by ourselves later. (And we do... but we miss the kids, too.) So we promised that everybody would get the top choice on their list, no matter what. All of us promised that we'd be tolerant of everyone else's first choice, even if we thought it was something we'd hate, in exchange for everyone else being tolerant of *our* first choice.

That gives everybody a stake in the success of the trip. A child (or a dad) who has helped plan a trip and knows he gets to see the No. 1 thing on his list is much less likely to whine or complain than somebody who's just dragged along.

2. Plan free time

Hardly anybody thinks about this until it's too late. On even a perfectly paced holiday, everyone is a lot more active than normal. You walk more and you stand on a lot of hard museum floors. You can forget that even pleasure travel is tiring and stressful with long car, train, or plane trips, crowded streets, and unfamiliar surroundings.

That's why it's important to actually schedule time to relax. You'll want to say, *"We're spending all this time and money to take this vacation and you expect us to spend a night just sitting in the hotel room in front of the TV?"*

Yep.

I also expect you to spend an afternoon in the park just lounging on the grass, an hour sitting on a bench at Rockefeller Plaza watching people skate, an evening on the Brooklyn Heights Promenade watching the sky get dark and the city light up, and a day just dozing in the sun on the Coney Island beach.

Maybe you won't do all those things, but all of you, kids and parents alike, *need* time to relax and recharge. If you keep yourself on the go all the time, you'll probably see more… but you'll enjoy it much less. It's hard to have fun when you're tired. A half day or evening of just loafing now and then will make the whole trip less intense and a lot more fun.

3. Keep your eating and sleeping on schedule

Another sound way to reduce the stress of travel is to keep as much as possible to your regular routine, something that's especially important to the youngest members of your family. Remember the travel axiom from earlier in the book: *The mood of the group is determined by its most tired member.*

While you'll certainly make exceptions for a few special activities, like seeing the city at night from the top of the Empire State Building, or going to a Broadway show, everyone will be happier if regular bedtimes are observed most of the time. And you stray from normal mealtimes only at your most dire peril!

If you're trying to decide whether to eat lunch before or after your visit to an attraction, remember that it's far, far better to eat a half hour too early than a half hour too late. Besides, if you eat just a bit early, you've got a built-in excuse to sit down and relax for a mid-afternoon snack.

Keeping Everyone Happy and Enthusiastic

Those three rules are basic. Do *not* violate them if you want everyone still speaking to each other when you get home! Here are three more suggestions. They don't carry the same force of law, but if peace, harmony, and an absence of grumbling are things you think improve a family vacation, give them very serious consideration. You'll thank me for them when you get home.

1. Observe the Two-Hour Rule

The Two-Hour Rule is simple: Don't spend more than two hours in any museum. Actually I think 90 minutes is better for a family, because somebody's bound to get bored, but you can't do justice to the American Museum of Natural History and a few other places in 90 minutes. On the other hand, you couldn't see the whole thing well in six hours, so spending more than two will just exhaust the people who don't care and frustrate those who do.

This suggestion applies mostly to museums and their hard floors. Some attractions beg for more than two hours. You can spend all day at Coney Island or in Central Park; they offer a wide and varied assortment of experiences. If you spend just two hours at a baseball game in Yankee Stadium, you'll probably leave in the sixth inning. But if you really *need* more than two hours in a particular museum, go back a second time.

2. Vary your activities

Avoid seeing two of the same kinds of attractions on the same day. The Metropolitan Museum of Art and the Guggenheim Museum are two of the great art museums of the world. They're not far apart and it's tempting to visit them both on the same day. Resist the temptation. That would diminish the grandeur of each.

The same is true for other pairs of activities like the views from the Empire State Building and World Trade Center, or two botanical gardens, or two grand cathedrals. Give each attraction its best chance to show itself to your family fresh and ready for the experience.

3. Split up occasionally
Do father and daughter want to go to a Mets' game while mother and son have their eyes on the Bronx Zoo? Do it! There's no reason why a family vacation means that every member of the family must spend every waking moment in the company of every other member of the family. This is supposed to be fun, after all! You'll want to do a lot of things together, of course, but sometimes the fun of an activity is doubled if only half the people go.

Let me take this a little further and make the parents just a little uneasy. If the kids are old enough, it's okay to let them head out on their own for awhile.

Alone in New York City? Sure. People do it all the time.

Make sure everybody knows basic rules of safety, knows how to get around comfortably on the subway, and has enough pocket money for a taxi in case they get hopelessly lost. But once you've been in the city for a few days, everyone will have a good feel for the place and will manage on their own perfectly well.

How old is old enough? That one you'll have to answer for yourself. I've known kids of 15 who were plenty old enough, and others much older that I wouldn't have trusted out of my sight if they'd been mine—which, fortunately, they weren't. But the teenager who sets out alone, or with a brother or sister, to conquer the big city, will have a lot more confidence, an interesting story or two, and a neat place he or she will want to show off to the others when you meet back at the hotel or apartment at dinnertime.

Recommendations

✔ Plan ahead, but be on the lookout for even more interesting things you weren't expecting.

✔ Follow the three rules of family travel, with a special commitment to the first one: Everybody gets their first choice.

✔ Don't be afraid to split up. It will give you twice as much to talk about that evening.

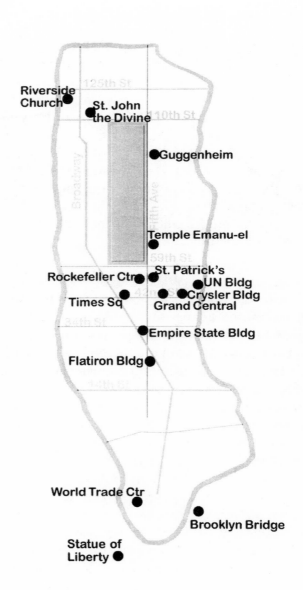

Chapter 10 Highlights

10. Stupendous Structures

Name the most famous structure in some of the world's greatest cities. Paris? Yes, the Eiffel Tower. London? Parliament and Big Ben, of course. Rome? St. Peter's. San Francisco? The Golden Gate Bridge, certainly. New York?

Uh—How do we choose?

Few cities can claim more than one or two truly distinctive structures, recognizable to people around the globe. New York has *way* more than its share. Its skyline is by far the most-photographed cityscape on the planet and almost any of the countless skyscrapers in midtown would be the pride of any other city. Here they just get lost. It's like trying to focus on each individual mountain in the Alps, or treat each tree in the Black Forest as something unique. Not a chance. If you're a millionaire, you don't pay attention to each bit of change in your pocket. So it is with buildings in New York.

All these architectural wonders are good for at least two things. First, they are fabulous just to look at, to marvel at the engineering feats required to build them. Almost as important, though, is their value to parents. When the kids get restless, challenge them to race to the top of the building or the end of the bridge... and let them win! Even the most rambunctious member of the younger generation will be a little more subdued for a while after climbing the Empire State Building.

The Lady with the Lamp

The Statue of Liberty is more than just a symbol of New York; it's one of the world's most familiar associations with the United States. Standing in New York Harbor, it's been the first vision of America for millions upon millions of immigrants to the country since 1886, and it's still one of the most popular attractions in the city.

The statue and base are more than 300 feet (93m) high, and if you (or the kids) have the wind for it, you can climb 354 steps to the crown. Visitors could once climb all the way up to the torch, but that last stage of the ascent has been closed for years because of concerns of structural damage. There's no elevator beyond the lower observation deck and museum (less than halfway up), and it's just as well, frankly, that the route to the torch is now closed. When you get to the crown, you are unlikely to be enthusiastic about the prospect of even more steps! It's the equivalent of climbing a 22-story building!

The Statue of Liberty has stood in New York Harbor for more than a hundred years

The wait in line can be very long on weekends and every day in the summer, but you can spend some time at the museum and observation deck instead. But if you're

Tip: To beat the crowds as much as possible, make this your first stop of the day. Boats leave Battery Park beginning at 9:30 A.M. If you arrive early enough to get on the first boat, it's the only waiting you'll have to do.

fit and not claustrophobic, the view of lower Manhattan from the crown is one of the most memorable in all New York.

If your wind, legs, courage, or patience aren't up to it, though, it's not necessary to climb to the top to enjoy the statue. Liberty Island is a wonderful place for a stroll, and the close views of the statue are something everyone will remember forever.

Since the same ferries go to the Statue of Liberty and to Ellis Island (Chapter 11), most visitors will stop at both places. And since generations of immigrants passed the statue on the way to admittance to the country through Ellis Island, it's worth noting that Lady Liberty is herself an immigrant. The statue was a gift from France. *[Liberty Island. Subway 1, 9: South Ferry; N, R: Whitehall St.; 4, 5: Bowling Green. Then ferry from Battery Park. Ticket booth is inside Castle Clinton]*

Reaching for the Skies

Whenever I fly into New York's LaGuardia Airport, I get a bit concerned about the pilot's ability to maintain control of the plane. The landing pattern often takes us over the skyscrapers of Manhattan, and all at once everyone on the plane is leaning in the same direction, straining to catch a glimpse of the famous skyline. Is this sudden weight shift going to send us into a spin?

Skyscrapers are the aristocrats of buildings. People all over the world recognize their names and photographs. Their sheer size makes them important, just as even a deposed monarch is accorded dignity and privilege. New York City has more architectural aristocrats than anywhere else in the world, but two stand out.

The Empire State Building

It's no longer the tallest building in the world—it's not even the tallest building in Manhattan any more—but the Empire State Building is the unchallenged king of tall buildings. It has been the centerpiece of movies from *King Kong* to *Sleepless in Seattle.* More than two million visitors a year stand on its observation decks peering 80 miles (130km) into the distance.

When my wife was a first grade teacher, one of the 6-year-olds looked at her with awe when she said she was taking a trip to New York. "Will you bring me a picture of the Empire State Building?" he begged her. We gave him one of our photos when we got back and he kept it on his desk for weeks.

We never understood just what *specific* attraction the building held for Jared, but we understand people's fascination with it. Its size is staggering. The building uses 73 elevators, running up and down 7 miles of shafts. Plumbers work on 60 miles of water pipes, telecom people on 3,500 miles of phone wires. Window washers never finish the 6,500 windows. Including the mast at the top, the building stands so tall at 1,454 feet (443m) that airplanes have crashed into its side and its top is sometimes visible above low clouds that obscure the middle.

Intrepid family members who want to walk up the steps to the 102nd-floor observation deck (1,250 feet up, about 380m) must climb 1,860 steps, although if you don't mind, I'll just take the high-speed elevator. The observation decks on the 86th and 102nd floors are open until midnight every day, and lines are shorter later in the evening, when the nighttime views of

The Empire State Building begins to light up at dusk

Manhattan are one of the most eye-popping sights in the world. *[Fifth Ave. at 34ᵗʰ St., Midtown. Subway B, D, F, N, Q, R: 34ᵗʰ St. Observation deck usually open until midnight]*

World Trade Center

Visitors sometimes don't realize it, because the Empire State Building gets all the publicity, but it's only the *third* tallest building in New York. The other two are the twin towers of the World Trade Center. The observation platform on Building 2 is 120 feet (37m) taller than that at the Empire State Building, and only fish have a better view of the ocean. Just riding the elevator to the top is fun— it takes less than a minute to zip you up to the 107ᵗʰ-floor indoor observation deck. But if the weather is nice, somebody will certainly insist on going up to the 110ᵗʰ-floor outdoor platform. It's quite an experience. It will be windy up there, but even the lightest family member need have no fear of being blown off.

The price is about double that at the Empire State Building but the crowds are smaller and lines to the elevator are shorter. But before you go up, check the signboard in the lobby to see what the day's visibility rating is.

The World Trade Center looms above Lower Manhattan

There's absolutely no point to paying the money to go up if clouds or fog obscure the view. If it's wind you want, just walking through the canyons formed by midtown skyscrapers will give you all you want—for free. *[2 World Trade Center, Lower Manhattan. Subway 1, 9, N, R: Cortland St.; E: World Trade Center. Open until 9:30 P.M. (11:30 P.M. summer). Under 5 free]*

Three Distinctive Places

Not every spectacular structure is a skyscraper. The sheer variety of extravagant edifices will amaze the kids and make Mom and Dad feel like they've fallen into an architect's Eden. Here are three more places that will take everyone's breath away.

Brooklyn Bridge

This masterpiece designed by engineer John Roebling and completed by his son in 1883, wasn't the world's first suspension bridge of this sort (Roebling built a smaller one in Cincinnati before he tackled Brooklyn), but it's arguably the most famous, the most photographed, and the most written about.

The Brooklyn Bridge is one of the city's best-known landmarks

Before the bridge went up, New York and Brooklyn were separate cities, and the only way to get from one to the other was by ferry across the East River. The bridge set the stage for the marriage of the cities and marked the true beginning of the world's greatest metropolis.

Stupendous Structures

A walk across the bridge is a great way to begin or end a day. The wooden walkway is about a mile long and runs down the middle of the bridge, almost 20 feet (6m) above the traffic, well protected from the cars and trucks. Engraved plates at the support towers give the history of the bridge and interesting facts about it, but instead of reading, most people gawk at the spectacular views of the Manhattan skyline and the geometric precision of the hundreds of cables that support the bridge. *[The pedestrian walkway begins in Manhattan at Center Street and Park Row, Lower Manhattan. Subway 4, 5, 6: Brooklyn Bridge-City Hall; J, M, Z: Chambers St. The Brooklyn end of the walkway begins at Tillary Street. Subway A, C, F: Jay St.-Borough Hall; M, N, R: Court St. Free]*

Grand Central Terminal

If in bygone years most immigrants to the United States landed at Ellis Island, most other new arrivals to New York came here, the grandest railroad station in America, Grand Central Terminal. After the great age of railways ended, though, and airplanes and automobiles took over the bulk of the transportation burden, the great station was allowed to decay. Fortunately, before the building was irretrievably lost, New York realized the architectural and historical treasure it had, and a refurbishment in the 1990s restored it to its original glory.

Now you can visit this gem, still a working station serving mostly commuters (a half million people per day!), and stand near the great clock in the center of its ticket hall, where countless lovers and families have agreed to meet and where hundreds of movie scenes have been filmed. The station houses dozens of cool places to eat and shop, but its centerpiece is its magnificent vaulted ceiling, deep sea green, with lights and gold leaf depicting thousands of stars and the constellations of the zodiac. You're sure to be in the area and it's worth at least a walkthrough. *[42nd St. and Park Ave., Midtown. Subway 4, 5, 6, 7, S: Grand Central. Free]*

Times Square is filled with cars and people 24 hours a day

Bright Lights of Times Square

It's hard to know where to put Times Square. My initial outline for the book listed it in five or six different chapters. We'll refer to it later in several other places, but I just have to talk about it here, at the beginning of this section of the book. Times Square isn't a *single* structure, but it's certainly stupendous! Nowhere else can you see the glitter and glamour, the bustle and buzz, the vigor and variety that are the hallmarks of New York City.

First there's the neon— acres and acres of neon, illuminating a plethora of signs that you can just stand and gawk at. Watch the giant Coke bottle drained of its contents, hour after hour. Speculate on how they make the steam come out of the giant cup of coffee or bowl of soup. Figure out what time it will be when the British soldier finally makes it into his guardhouse on the Virgin Airlines billboard. It's almost as good as watching television.

Oh, yes. Television. You can watch TV on gigantic screens, high above the busy streets. Follow the news or stock market on enormous illuminated tickers. Listen to calypso bands and street preachers on the corners. Buy giant pretzels or fat sausages to snack on from sidewalk carts. Pet the horses of the mounted policemen who patrol the area. Shop curbside tables for wristwatches that work for a week, sun-glasses that crack in a day, and bootleg copies of popular CDs.

Every street in the area is filled with lots to do. In 1990, 42nd Street was a place you wouldn't have considered taking your family. Now it's a wonderland. The Disney organization has sunk millions of dollars into renovating the classic New Amsterdam Theatre and that's led to the redevelopment of the entire street. Now it's filled with theaters, arcades, restaurants—even a branch of the famous Madam Tussaud's wax museum.

There's fun and activity in Times Square all day long—and most of the night, too. You'll wonder where all the stretch limos come from and just who's behind the tinted glass windows. You'll hear passersby speaking practically every language known to humanity. You'll see stores packed with goods you think you can't afford, until you start to walk out. (I looked at a tool marked $89 one evening and decided it was much more than I

Plan to spend some time in Times Square

was willing to pay. The salesman first cut the price to $59, then $39, finally $19.95. I guess the moral here is the same as with hotels: Don't pay rack rate!)

If you get hungry while you're here, you're within a ten-minute walk of probably 250 restaurants serving every imaginable cuisine at prices from less than $2 per person to more than $200 each.

And of course, anyone in your family who loves George Selden's wonderful children's novel *The Cricket in Times Square* will insist on ducking into the subway here to look for the newsstand home of Chester Cricket. It's just one more reason for making this an early stop on your trip.

Going to Times Square is like going to the circus. All it needs is elephants. *[Technically Times Square is where Broadway, 42nd St., and Seventh Ave. converge, but in practice it's the area along Broadway between 42nd and 50th streets, Midtown. Subway: 16 lines serve the area]*

More Than You Have Time For!

New York has so much architectural glitz that we might have fallen into a chapter that will never end. Maybe we'll just hopscotch through some of the other places on the list. All are worth discovering and savoring. Many will be destinations on your list and others you'll just stumble across. Some, perhaps, you wouldn't have known about but for this chapter and will be inspired to seek out. Let's take a quick look at a few more possibilities.

Buildings Galore

Each of these is a feast for the eyes. Not all are skyscrapers, but each will make you catch your breath with its uniqueness and daring. And Oh! what I've had to leave out!

The **Chrysler Building** *[405 Lexington Ave. at E. 42nd St., Midtown. Subway 4, 5, 6, 7, S: Grand Central. Closed Saturday and Sunday. No observation deck but a walk through the lobby is free]* is an Art Deco masterpiece, one of the finest and gaudiest examples of this early twentieth-century style. The lobby with its inlays, chrome, and polished wood highlights, was once an automobile showroom. This was the world's tallest building in 1930—until the Empire State Building was finished a few months later.

Also the tallest building in the world when it was finished in 1903, the **Flatiron Building** [*175 Fifth Ave. at Broadway and W. 23rd St., Chelsea. Subway N, R: 23rd St. Closed Saturday and Sunday. Free*] is probably my favorite building in New York. There's no real reason to go inside, but everybody will enjoy looking at its odd triangular shape and speculating what it would be like to live in an apartment at the pointed end. Madison Square Park across the street is a perfect vantage point and a nice place to sit and relax.

Chapter 15 will provide more information about Frank Lloyd Wright's masterpiece, the **Guggenheim Museum** [*1071 Fifth Ave. at E. 89th St., Upper East Side. Subway 4, 5, 6: 86th St.*]. But even if you're not a lover of modern art, you'll love this tall white spiral building. One of the kids is sure to suggest how cool it would be to skateboard or scooter his way down the coil of galleries.

More than a single building, **Rockefeller Center** [*47th to 52nd streets along Fifth and Sixth avenues, Midtown. Subway B, D, F, S: Rockefeller Ctr.*] is a 22-acre complex of nineteen buildings covering ten square blocks. The huge *G.E. Building* and *Radio City Music Hall* are probably the best known landmarks, but a quarter of a million people work throughout this city within a city. The complex is at its finest around Christmastime, when ice skaters fill the skating rink beneath an enormous Christmas tree, pirouetting, waltzing, and colliding to holiday music. You can rent skates there if you left yours at home.

They aren't the tallest buildings in the world, but the buildings that make up the **United Nations** [*First Ave. at E. 46th St., Midtown. Subway 4, 5, 6, 7, S: Grand Central*] are surely among the most important. The next chapter will go into more detail, but even if you don't take a tour, it's worth your time to stop here and admire the striking buildings where the people of the world meet to try to resolve their differences.

Divine Houses of Worship
Churches throughout the world provide some of the most dramatic and daring of all buildings. New York City has a surplus of such places. If you're a churchgoing family, by all means visit the principal church of your denomination in the city. But even if you're not religious, you'll find secular inspiration in some of these houses of worship.

Under construction for more than a century and still decades from completion, the **Cathedral of St. John the Divine** *[Amsterdam Ave. and W. 112th St., Upper West Side. Subway 1, 9, B, C: Cathedral Pkwy (110th) St. Free]* will someday be the largest Episcopal cathedral in the world and second only to St. Peter's Basilica in Rome among all houses of worship.

Ten blocks further north in the Morningside Heights area of the Upper West Side is **Riverside Church** *[490 Riverside Dr. at W. 120th St., Upper West Side. Subway 1, 9: 116th St.; A, B, C, D: 125th St. Free]*. This huge church's carillon, bells, and pipe organ are among the largest in the world. For an unrivaled view of northern Manhattan, take the elevator to the 20th floor of the bell tower and walk up another long flight of steps to the observation platform.

The best-known church in New York is probably **St. Patrick's Cathedral** *[Fifth Ave. at 50th St., Midtown. Subway E, F: 53rd St. Free]*, the largest and most important Catholic church in the United States. Popes have prayed in its ornate Gothic interior.

Built in 1929, **Temple Emanu-el** *[1 E. 65th St. at Fifth Ave., Upper East Side. Subway 6: 68th St. Free]* is one of the largest synagogues in the world, seating more than 2,000 people.

Ornate Hotels

Some of the most opulent buildings in town are its hotels. Even if you can't afford to stay there, walk through the ornate crystal and marble lobbies of the **Plaza Hotel** *[768 Fifth Ave. at Central Park South, Midtown. Subway N, R, W: 5th Ave.; S: 57th St.]* and the **Waldorf Astoria** *[301 Park Ave. at 49th St., Midtown. Subway 6: 51st St.].*

While you're in the Times Square area, you might stop at the **Marriott Marquis** *[45th St. and Broadway, Midtown. All Times Square area subways].* Go up to its eighth-floor lobby and gaze in amazement at the largest hotel atrium in the world. The kids will insist on taking the glass elevator up the center of the atrium all the way to the top, more than 40 stories up. But don't make fun of anyone who prefers to face the elevator door instead. It's a bit scary.

Recommendations

✔ The Empire State Building is worth two trips: one during the day for the phenomenal view and one at night for the spectacular lights.

✔ Times Square is worth two trips: one during the day for the activity and bustle and one at night for the spectacular lights.

✔ If you don't go out to the Statue of Liberty, you'll regret it later.

✔ Avail yourselves of every opportunity for New York's breathtaking views—from building tops, bridges, church towers, down the streets splitting rows of gargantuan buildings. Nowhere else in the world has views like this.

✔ Pay attention to the architecture and ornamentation of the buildings you pass as you walk. Challenge the kids to pick out the little details most people miss.

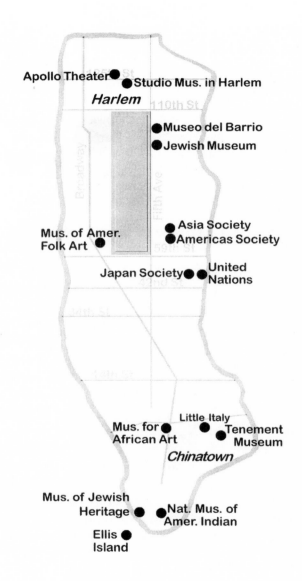

Chapter 11 Highlights

11. Cross-Cultural Corners

WHEEL OF NATIONS

If America is the world's melting pot, New York City is where the ingredients are usually added. That "melting pot" term gets tossed around a lot, but few people stop to think what it means. Melt several ingredients together and the result is more than just a combination of the components—you've got something entirely new, completely different from the things that went into it, more than the sum of its parts. Combine copper and tin and you have bronze—stronger and more durable than either. Combine chocolate and caramel and you have—well, I don't know what it's called, but it's wonderful.

And if you combine all the people of the world, you have New York—strong and spicy, a culture like nowhere else on the planet. There's no better reason for bringing *your* family to New York City than to show that cultural diversity not only works, it enriches everyone. If we could only do on the global level what 8 million people have done here!

The World Capital

I said in the book's introduction that if Planet Earth had a capital city, it would surely be New York City. Well, in a sense, New York *is* the capital of the world. The most altruistic organization in world history, the United Nations, has its headquarters here. This assembly of nearly all the world's countries is devoted to bringing peace and respect among all the peoples of the earth. Even though it has not yet succeeded, the effort itself is among the noblest of all human enterprises. On a family trip to New York, you can see these peacemakers at work.

Oddly enough, though, in order to visit the United Nations, you must leave the United States.

Don't be confused. The 14-acre UN complex that stretches for six blocks along the East River *is* surrounded by New York City, but it technically is not part of the United States. It is independent territory, belonging to the United Nations itself. It

even has its own post office and issues its own stamps, which can be used to mail letters *only* from UN headquarters in New York and its offices in Geneva and Vienna.

When you visit the UN, spend a little while in the gardens adjacent to the building before you go in; they set the mood brilliantly. Pass the colorful line of flags (Each member's flag is displayed in English alphabetical order) and cross the broad plaza to enter the gardens.

Aside from being a wonderfully peaceful respite from the traffic nearby, and providing

Peace is the dominant theme of the sculpture outside the UN building

stunning views of the East River, Queens, Roosevelt Island, and the Queensboro Bridge, the gardens are filled with sculpture that speaks to the ideal of the organization. One of my favorite pieces is "Good

Tip: *Like most security people, guards here will assure you that the x-rays will not harm your film and will be reluctant to just hand inspect it. But if you have your film in the lead bag you use for air travel, you'll be protected from x-rays and will get the hand inspection you want.*

Defeats Evil," which looks very like St. George slaying the dragon. It was a gift of the former Soviet Union and is made from pieces of Russian and American nuclear missiles that were destroyed as part of a 1987 treaty.

The visitors' entrance is in the middle of the plaza. You will be asked to have your bags x-rayed and will pass through a metal detector, but cameras are permitted and photos are allowed everywhere except in rooms where a meeting is in progress.

Guided tours are frequent, and offered in many languages. (The UN has six official languages: Arabic, Chinese, English, French, Russian, and Spanish.) You'll pass along corridors filled with art from all over the world as your guide explains the history and workings of the organization. Best of all, you can enter the great halls where meetings are held, including the two best-known: the Security Council chamber with its great round table, where the gravest decisions are made about war and peace in the world; and the General Assembly, the one place where nearly all the countries of the Earth come together to discuss and debate. You might even be lucky enough to be present during a meeting, as I was on one trip, and see the Secretary-General at work. [First Avenue at E. 46th St., Midtown. Subway 4, 5, 6, 7, S: Grand Central. Tours are available every day except weekends in Jan. and Feb.]

Melting Pot Ingredients

It's not true that all the flavors in American society were added to the mix in New York City. Native Americans were here before anybody else, of course. African slaves were not immigrants, they were brought as prisoners. Asian newcomers more often entered through California than New York.

Still, bloodlines mix, and it might be hard today to find a family—inside *or* outside the United States—that didn't have relatives or friends emigrate to the U.S., entering their new homes through New York City. Where Europeans—or Americans of European ancestry are concerned—the probability becomes a virtual certainty.

New York City, more than most U.S. cities, remembers and celebrates that legacy. If you have any interest in that heritage, New York has a couple of wonderful places to visit.

Ellis Island

From 1892 until 1954, the first stop for most immigrants to the United States was a small island in New York Harbor—Ellis Island. New arrivals were questioned here, given medical examinations and, if they were able to satisfy the inspectors that they were healthy, of good character, and able to be self-supporting, they were admitted to the country.

A few ill passengers were confined to hospitals on the island tempoarily. A handful, about 2 percent, were refused entry and deported, mostly because of infectious diseases or criminal pasts in their homelands. But 12 million people entered the United States here, and their descendents now number many, many times that.

It's worth noting that the immigrants processed at Ellis Island were mostly the poorest of the new arrivals. Ships' passengers who could afford first- or second-class tickets went through their inspections on board and didn't have to endure the rigors of Ellis Island's Registry Room, which often processed 5,000 people per day. Particularly in the early days of the facility, passengers were taken advantage of, bilked of their few possessions, and frightened into offering bribes. By the early twentieth cen-

> ***Tip:*** *Ferries from Battery Park stop at Liberty Island, then continue to Ellis Island. Go to the Statue of Liberty first thing in the morning, then take a ferry from there to Ellis Island for a visit. Your ferry ticket covers stops at both islands.*

tury the process had been largely cleaned up, but it was still an intimidating place.

Today you can follow the first steps your great-grandfather or an uncle took on American soil. The exhibits are interesting and evocative. See cases of treasured possessions brought from all over the world, lost or abandoned here. Listen to taped reminiscences of immigrants, talking about their aspirations and entry into the country. Inspect dozens of native costumes and scores of boxes and trunks—all that many people owned.

Ellis Island was the first taste of America for 12 million immigrants

Peer into a dormitory room, cots covering every bit of floor space, stacked three tiers high, where detainees waited to learn their fates. I was much more moved by the cumulative effect than I expected to be. Younger children might not get much out of the visit—but teens and their parents will. *[Subway 1, 9, N, R: South Ferry; 4, 5: Bowling Green. Then ferry from Battery Park. Ticket booth is inside Castle Clinton]*

Lower East Side Tenement Museum
Once they had cleared the obstacles of Ellis Island, new arrivals were faced with the even more daunting prospect of deciding what to do next. Many immediately boarded trains for other parts of the country where relatives were waiting. But countless thousands went no further than a few blocks, blending into New York's vast slums and blocks of crowded tenements. One of the most unusual museums in the city provides a stirring look at the way they lived.

The Lower East Side of Manhattan absorbed wave after wave of immigrants—Chinese, Irish, Italian, Jews from Germany and Eastern Europe, Poles, and more. Now, in a building that,

Crowded tenements on the Lower East Side were the first homes of many new Americans

between 1863 and 1935, housed more than 7,000 people from more than 20 nations, you can see how those diverse people survived in their new land. The Tenement Museum offers tours through some of the crowded apartments that housed up to 20 people at a time without the benefit of running water or indoor toilets. Guides will take you on walks through the neighborhoods that have been America's most ethnically varied area, where you can hold conversations with costumed interpreters recreating the lives of the people who lived here. The museum also offers a wide array of special programs from cooking to crafts that take visitors back more than a century to view dimensions of the changing cultures that created a vibrant city.

For anybody interested in history or immigration, this museum is a gem that's far off the usual tourist tracks. *[90 Orchard St. at Broome St., Lower East Side. Subway F, J, M, Z: Delancey St. Closed Monday]*

Ethnic Enclaves

It's simply not possible to categorize all the ethnic neighborhoods in New York City. Astoria, in Queens, has a large Greek community. Long Island City in Queens has both Korean and Philippine neighborhoods. Brooklyn's Brighton Beach has a strong Russian flavor. Little Brazil is in midtown Manhattan, East Harlem is Hispanic—you get the idea. Many groups settled first on the Lower East Side, but have found their own urban niches elsewhere.

Not surprisingly, you can see remnants of many of those early populations. Lots of visitors head for **Little Italy**, not far west of the Tenement Museum, expecting the authentic flavor of old New York. Well, you'll find a lot of flavors: It's a tasty place to eat Italian food. But inhabitants are more likely to be the upwardly mobile white collar crowd now. If you want to find New York City's largest Italian community, you'll have to visit **Carroll Gardens** in Brooklyn. One son who lived there for

> **Tip:** *Stop for a treat at the China-town Ice Cream Factory, 65 Bayard St., for delicious treats you've never had before. Try red bean ice cream, or a lichee nut cone.*

awhile said it was kind of like finding himself in an old 1930s black-and-white movie—Mama leaning from the window, shouting with a heavy Italian accent to the kids playing in the street, "You get up here and wash for supper before your Papa gets home!" When I visited, that's exactly what I found.

Chinatown [*Subway 6, J, M, N, Q, R, W, Z: Canal St.*], south of Canal Street and east of Broadway, is much more authentic, on the other hand; it's virtually a separate city, with a population of 100,000 people. It's fun to elbow your way through crowded Canal Street, or wander along *slightly* quieter Mulberry or Mott streets, looking at the colorful red and gold signs and fanciful roofs. Kids will stare at some remarkably ugly fish, wide-eyed atop piles of ice in local markets, and will pick up souvenir copies of Chinese newspapers with their pages of indecipherable characters (to Western eyes, that is) running vertically down the page.

The colorful streets and shops of Chinatown provide great walking, shopping, and eating

Everyone will enjoy going into stores and looking at the unfamiliar wares—or at Chinese versions of familiar things. And you *definitely* want to visit Chinatown at mealtime! If you want to know more about the area, visit the **Museum of Chinese in the Americas** *[70 Mulberry St., Chinatown. Subway 6, J, M, N, Q, R, W, Z: Canal St. Open Tues-Sat afternoons. Under 12 free]* where you'll learn the history of New York's Chinatown and of Chinese immigration to America. The museum is on the second floor. There's no sign outside. Enter the building and look for the sign next to the stairway.

While everybody enjoys Chinatown, there's one neighborhood in Manhattan that it's difficult to get tourists to visit. It's a shame, because **Harlem**, the historic center of New York City's African-American community, is a pleasure to stroll. You'll find the same sort of brownstones here you will on the much more fashionable Upper East Side, and if you don't find the same exclusive shops, you'll at least find lower prices and be able to wander for blocks in the sunshine, unobscured by skyscrapers. I'll just add that I find far more shoppers on 125th Street smile and nod hello as I pass than I've *ever* found on Madison Avenue.

The decision of former U.S. president Bill Clinton to locate his personal office in the heart of Harlem will probably lead to more development and more visitors in the area, but the fact is, the rediscovery of Harlem by white Manhattanites was already well underway. The area around 125th Street and Lenox Avenue, always an entertainment center anchored by the **Apollo Theater**, is now filled with clubs and restaurants, and with lots of inexpensive places to shop for the latest music and cool clothes. One of the very nicest galleries in the city, the **Studio Museum in Harlem** at 144 W. 125th St. *[closed Mon. & Tues.]*, provides space and a variety of programming devoted to minority artists. *[For a walk through Harlem, take Subway 1, 2, 3, 4, 5, 6, A, B, C, D to 125th St.]*

Museum Heritage

I've seen dozens of guidebooks to New York (and have even written one) and haven't yet seen one that lists *all* the museums. It's impossible, I suppose, because they come and go. But I'll make the point repeatedly that if you're interested in something, New York probably has a museum devoted to it. That's true of the peoples, cultures, and religions that make up this great city.

Here is a selection of some of the most interesting museums of ethnic culture or art I've found in the city. If you want to investigate your own heritage, or teach your kids more about the marvelous diversity of the world's people, these might be good starting points.

The **National Museum of the American Indian** [*1 Bowling Green, Lower Manhattan. Subway 4, 5: Bowling Green. Free*], a branch of the Smithsonian, is quartered in one of the neatest buildings in the city. Built as the Custom House, in 1900, the building received the revenues from all the tariffs paid on goods imported into the United States. Palatial inside and out, the fabulous elliptical rotunda is almost worth the trip in itself. Since 1994, however, the building has held an important national collection of Native American relics and artifacts. I was especially drawn in by the clothing, far more decorative and ornate than the way it's usually depicted in the popular media.

El Museo del Barrio [*1230 Fifth Ave. at 104th St., Upper East Side. Subway 6: 103rd St. Closed Mon. & Tues.*] celebrates the heritage of Puerto Rican and other Latin American cultures in the United States with an extensive collection of Latin art and artifacts that date back to pre-Columbian times.

The **Museum of Jewish Heritage** [*18 First Place, Battery. Subway 1, 9: South Ferry; 4, 5: Bowling Green; N, R: Whitehall St. Closed Sat.*] is a modern, pyramid-shaped building that tells the story of Jewish history. The first floor focuses on Jewish culture and tradition. The second floor tells the story of Jewish persecution, particularly the Holocaust. You cannot fail to be moved by artifacts salvaged from the death camps, the hundreds of haunting photographs, and the taped reminiscences of its survivors. The third floor discusses modern Jewish life and the formation of Israel, and features a lounge with large windows looking out over New York Harbor and the Statue of Liberty. The **Jewish Museum** *[1109 Fifth Ave. at 92nd St., Upper East Side. Subway 6: 96th St. Closed Fri. & Sat. Under 12 free]* on the Upper East Side has more extensive collections of traditional Jewish religion and culture, including many archeological treasures.

There is almost no end to the cultural museums, galleries, and exhibits in New York. A few more:

The **Museum for African Art** *[593 Broadway at Houston St., Soho. Subway N, R: Prince St. Closed Mon.]*

The **Museum of American Folk Art** *[Columbus Ave. at W. 66th St., Upper West Side. Subway: 1, 9: 66th St.-Lincoln Center. Closed Mon. Free]*

The **Americas Society** *[680 Park Ave. at 68th St., Upper East Side. Subway 6: 68th St. Closed Mon. Free]* covers all of the Western Hemisphere outside the United States.

The **Asia Society** *[725 Park Ave. at 70th St., Upper East Side. Subway 6: 68th St. Closed Mon.]*

The **Japan Society Gallery** *[333 E. 47thSt. between First & Second avenues, Midtown. Subway 6: 51st St. Closed Mon.]*

Wherever your family goes in New York City, you will be reminded of the richness of human culture. As far as I'm concerned, that's one of the very best reasons to visit.

Recommendations

✔ Spend a day exploring your own family's heritage, or that of another nationality or ethnic group.

✔ One evening back in your apartment or hotel, spend an hour listening to the radio. In how many languages can you find programming in New York City?

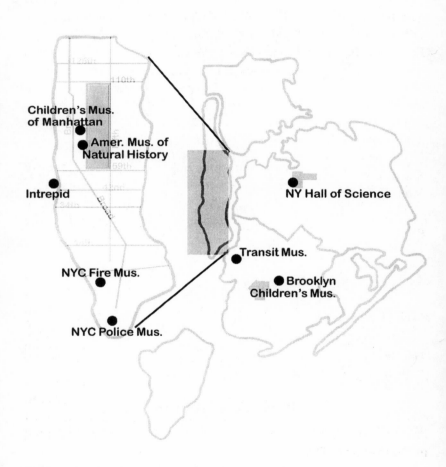

Children's Mus.
of Manhattan

Amer. Mus. of
Natural History

Intrepid

NY Hall of Science

NYC Fire Mus.

Transit Mus.

Brooklyn
Children's Mus.

NYC Police Mus.

Chapter 12 Highlights

12. *Magnificent Museums*

There's a lot to like about museums. For one thing, they're a refuge. On a backbreakingly hot New York summer day, they can be as cool as lemonade. In the cold wind of January they are toasty and comfortable. They're dry when the rain outside pours down.

Besides, they're filled with neat stuff.

We *love* museums—museums packed with glass cases containing ancient or mysterious objects; museums dedicated to just a single theme, but that tell you everything and more than you could possibly want to know about it; and best of all, museums that let you discover things for yourself, places where you can get your hands dirty (sometimes literally!) with science or art. New York has all that and more. One of the finest walks in the city is **Museum Mile**, the stretch of Fifth Avenue between 82nd and 105th streets, where you'll find more splendid museums in less space than anywhere else in the country except the Mall in Washington, D.C.

Almost every chapter in Part II of this book describes museums that will delight somebody in your family. Here are some worth separating out because of their broad appeal to kids. The first of these is a "don't miss" attraction for every family, the second should appeal to virtually everybody, and the others will be a highlight of the trip for kids of the right age or interest.

The book offers repeated advice not to overdo museums... but some things are worth overdoing.

The Natural World

Wherever we've traveled, one of our first museum stops is at a natural history or science museum: Chicago's Field Museum and Museum of Science and Industry; London's Science and Natural History museums; in Paris the Musée National d'Histoire Naturelle and Cité des Sciences et de l'Industrie; several of Washington's Smithsonian museums. New York isn't left behind in this category, either. You're in for a treat.

American Museum of Natural History
If there's a museum anywhere in the city that will make you want to violate the Two-Hour Rule, this must be it. The AMNH is packed with more than 32 million specimens and artifacts. This is a museum that can absorb as much time as you want to give it. But you *can* see the highlights in two hours, then go back another day if you want more.

It's hard, though, to know where to start. It's tempting to go in the entrance on Central Park West and see the great dinosaurs in the rotunda, then move up to the fourth floor for two huge rooms full of the big lizards, plus an exhibition of other extinct animals.

Maybe you'd rather enter on 77th Street, though, and take a look at the huge Indian war canoe—64 feet long (19.6m). From there you can go straight ahead to one of the country's most comprehensive exhibits of Native American life, or turn left to the country's best exhibition devoted to human origins and evolution. Beyond that is the hall of meteorites (including the largest one ever found), and then a dazzling exhibition of gems and minerals, including the Star of India, the world's largest blue-star sapphire.

What else? Well, there's a 94-foot-long (28.7m) replica of a blue whale suspended above the Ocean Life gallery, exhibits about vast arrays of the peoples and animals of the world, a four-story-tall Imax theater, and the renowned Hayden Planetarium, the most technologically advanced planetarium in the world, heart of an all-new astronomy and astrophysics facility.

The AMNH is a place of superlatives. There are few places like it in the world. *[21 Central Park West at 79th St., Upper West Side. Subway B, C: 81st St. Closed Mon.]*

New York Hall of Science
You'll find no glass cases here. This is one of the finest science education museums I've ever seen—and most tourists miss it because it's not in Manhattan. If there was ever a reason to get into the boroughs, this is it. Even the building, built for the 1964 World's Fair, is gorgeous, from its bright domed entry to its Great Hall with walls of blue stained glass.

Everything here is devoted to discovery, exploration, and learning, and it's especially ideal for kids up through early high school. Everything is hands-on. One of the first things you see in the exhibit hall is a glucose molecule enlarged a quadrillion times (that's 1,000,000,000,000,000 if you're counting) that serves as an introduction to chemistry and biology. Here kids can perform experiments that show them how their senses work, how the chemical components that make up their bodies are the same ones that make up kittens, cockroaches, and spinach, even find out how many people with a genetic makeup similar to theirs have visited the museum.

In the Sound exhibit, kids can use computers to create bird-call symphonies, original jazz compositions, and shadows that play music. In fact, the whole museum is packed with easy-to-use technology, from thermal sensors that give kids a picture of what's going on inside their bodies to microscopes that even *I* can see things in. It's all here—astronomy, optics, biology…

a marvelous list that even includes a radio station and computers with free Internet access. "Explainers" in red aprons are everywhere. These are high school and college students who keep everybody involved and answer questions. The museum has a special preschool area where an Explainer helps the littlest members of your family discover science principles.

Outside from April through November is the museum's 30,000 square foot playground, the largest science playground in the Western Hemisphere, with dozens of outdoor toys and games that teach through play. In fact, that's the hallmark of the entire museum: It offers so much fun that kids don't ever realize they're learning.

The museum has fascinating special exhibitions, too. Recent ones include a special focus on women's health and one on the science behind sports. *[47-01 111ᵗʰ St., Queens. Subway 7: 111ᵗʰ St. Open every day but closes at 2 P.M. Mon.]*

For the Young At Heart

I wish we had visited New York City when our kids were small, because I know two places they would have loved. It's too late for us (although the next generation may be visiting before long) but if *your* kids are still in the 2 to 10 age range, you and they might find the next page or two interesting.

These two children's museums are missed by most tourists, who are lured elsewhere by more famous attractions. For the youngest tourists, though, the children's museums of Manhattan and Brooklyn might well be a more memorable stop than anything else you do. Their size, scale, and attractions are designed with little ones in mind.

Children's Museum of Manhattan
How would you like to crawl into somebody's mouth and up the tongue? Make somebody's muscles jump and twitch? Squeeze through somebody's small intestine?

No, I wouldn't either. But kids would probably think that was pretty neat, and here's the place they can do it. In this special corner of the city, it's hard to tell the learning from the play, and that's just what pint-size museum-goers love about the Children's Museum.

You can enter the world of Dr. Suess here, wandering through his slightly off-center universe while listening to his verse and looking at his original drawings. Or direct and act in your very own TV show, produced in the museum's private television studio. On one visit I entered Mister Rogers' Neighborhood, straight from the beloved television series. Kids could open a closet and put on a sweater, while seeing Mr. Rogers' own sweater and sneakers, as well as the trolley and King Friday's castle. Another temporary e x h i b i t i o n celebrated the 50th anniversary of the Peanuts comic strip.

There's a party room, art studio, and even a baby room with big soft shapes to play with. The whole museum is packed with things to climb, projects to build,

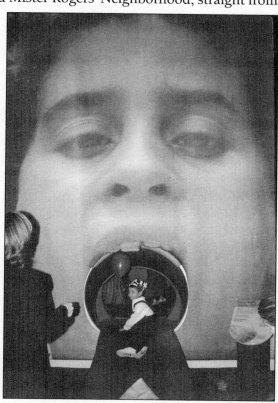

Kids will be swallowed up by the Children's Museum of Manhattan

AMERICAN KID
(INFANS AMERICANUS)

Be sure to visit a children's museum in Manhattan or Brooklyn

music to make, art to create, all done with care, sensitivity, and a sense of whimsy; you'll find no "Do Not Enter" signs here, for example. Instead, you might see a sign that says *"Bad Door. Until this door apologizes for being annoying, it cannot be in the exhibition."*

It's a lovely place. [212 W. 83rd St., Upper West Side. Subway 1, 9: 79th St. Closed Mon. and Tues. (closed only on Mon. in July and Aug.)]

Brooklyn Children's Museum

Hard to believe a children's museum could be any better than that, but maybe you could try the one in Brooklyn before you decide. The BCM is another great reason not to confine yourself to Manhattan. This is the oldest children's museum in the world, founded in 1899.

Visitors have access to a nonstop array of programs and workshops ranging from "bubbology" (You won't believe what you can do with bubbles!) to uses for tree bark. The museum has ten galleries of hands-on exhibits, live animals, geography, and map-making. You might find a kid-size tunnel with a waterwheel and stream, a computer and video room with interactive games and a miniature town, a pizzeria, dance studio, clubhouse—plus wonderful temporary exhibitions, like the set from the popular children's TV show *Sesame Street*.

The museum plays host on summer Friday evenings to an array of live performances from comedy to West African drumming to folk dancing, and special craft workshops for 5-and-unders are a regular part of the afternoon schedule.

Getting to the museum in the summertime is almost the best part of the experience. The Brooklyn Trolley runs every hour on weekends, making stops at the Grand Army Plaza near Prospect Park and the Brooklyn Museum of Art. *[145 Brooklyn Ave., Brooklyn. Subway 3: Kingston Ave. Closed Mon. and Tues. (closed only on Mon. in July and Aug.)*

Out of the Ordinary

You can find science museums everywhere (although few as good as the ones above) and children's museums exist in other places. New York has lots more choices, though, which are less common. If the phrase "something for everyone" weren't so trite, I'd be tempted to use it in referring to the city's selection of museums. So let's take a look at a few more especially neat places to visit.

Intrepid Sea Air Space Museum
Here's your chance to wander through a genuine aircraft carrier. This 900-foot-long (275m) warship served in the U.S. Navy from 1943 to 1973 and was home to as many as 3,400 men and more than 100 airplanes. It's been moored off midtown Manhattan as a floating museum since 1982. Exhibits aboard the ship show how it survived kamikaze and torpedo attacks during World War II, led bombing raids in Vietnam, and served as the prime recovery ship for NASA's early Mercury and Gemini space flights.

Visitors have the run of most of the ship, although a few remote areas are off limits because of safety concerns, but you'll undoubtedly spend most of your time on the bridge, on deck, and on the enormous hangar deck, where you can see fighter planes from several countries and the enormous elevators that took planes to the surface for launch. Also included in the admission price are tours of the missile submarine *Growler* and the destroyer *Edson*, which are berthed next to the carrier.

[W. 46th St. and 12th Ave., Midtown. Nearest subways are those at Times Square, a 15-minute walk; a No. 50 bus runs along 49th St. and stops in front of the museum. Closed Mon. and Tues. Oct. through Mar.; otherwise open daily]

One of the city's hottest places is the **NYC Fire Museum** *[278 Spring St., Soho. Subway C, E: Spring St. Closed Sun. and Mon.].* It's filled with fire-fighting equipment and apparatus dating back more than 200 years, including horse-drawn fire wagons, old uniforms and helmets (can you imagine a brigade of firemen in top hats?), safety equipment, even toys. The building itself is a hundred-year-old firehouse. The museum is uncrowded, unless a school group happens to be touring, and the staff (mostly firefighters themselves) are always happy to explain the exhibits and tell stories.

If you'd like a taste of the *real* police in New York, instead of those you see on TV, visit the **New York City Police Museum** *[25 Broadway, Battery. Subway 4, 5: Bowling Green].* The museum contains large displays of badges, uniforms and weapons of the

The NYC Fire Museum is full of old uniforms and equipment

past and present and a good display devoted to notorious criminals. You can inspect police cars and motorcycles... and even Al Capone's submachine gun. Special displays highlight the station house, detective and forensic work, and drug awareness. Visitors at least 18 years old can even try the firearms training simulator, but if anyone in your group is misbehaving, I don't think they'll lock them up for you.

If you enjoy riding the city's subways and buses, ride on over to the **New York Transit Museum** [*Boerum Pl. and Schermerhorn St., Brooklyn. Subway 2, 3, 4, 5: Borough Hall; M, N, R: Court St. Closed Mon.*]. If you don't know the difference between the BMT and IRT subway lines (though, honestly, there's no reason for visitors to care), this is the place to learn that and much more. The museum displays virtually every type of subway car ever used in New York. The oldest (circa 1878) is Car 41, later armored and converted into a money train, which until 1955 went from station to station collecting money from the ticket booths. There's a terrific exhibit on how the subway was built, an incredible engineering feat, and displays of signs, maps, and tokens. There's a new exhibit of model trains and lots of detail on how the world's most complicated system of public transportation works. There are a lot of steps to climb, because much of the museum is actually in the subway system itself.

Recommendations

✔ Don't confine yourself just to Manhattan. Some of New York City's finest museums are in the boroughs.

✔ If you have little ones along, a visit to one of the children's museums will provide a slower-paced but very satisfying afternoon.

✔ Stroll down Museum Mile, but remember that some of New York's most interesting museums are located in odd corners of the city. Think of yourself as a temporary New Yorker, not a tourist, and seek them out.

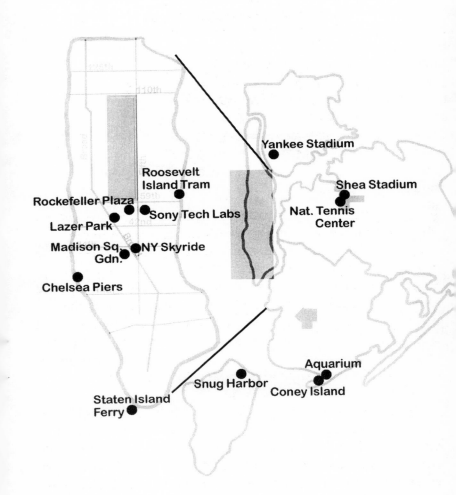

Chapter 13 Highlights

13. Family Fun

AQUARIUM BREAK ROOM

Certainly New York City has problems. But frankly, the biggest one you're likely to encounter is the one that no mayor will ever solve: There's just too much to do!

Our own family travels have taken us to a lot of places. Some were great museum towns, but with little to do in the evening. Some were places with lovely walks and views but with no sense of history or culture. And we still sometimes talk about the city where the main museum we wanted to visit was closed for good and where there was nothing else at all going on. We spent a very nice rainy night there playing cards in a hotel room, however—the only game in town, as they say.

No chance of that in New York!

This chapter will touch on just a few of the countless out-of-the-ordinary things to do in the city, things that don't easily fit into any of the other, more thematic, chapters. Oh, if you look, you can find much more. But here are some fun places to start, including some no ordinary out-of-towner would think about.

Coney Island

I don't know why tourists don't go out to the boroughs beyond Manhattan. The atmosphere is much different and the attractions are—I don't want to say more genuine—but the real historic New York. For a great summertime break from the traffic and tall buildings, do what generations of New Yorkers have done: Spend an afternoon and evening playing at Coney Island.

Kids love this place, and why not? You've got all the usual beach attractions of sun, sand, and sea, but you've also got the very prototype of the amusement park right at hand. Before there was Disneyworld, before there was Six Flags—there was Coney Island. Oh, Coney isn't the place it was in its heyday. The original three amusement parks (Steeplechase Park in 1897, Luna Park in 1903, Dreamland in 1904) were the first of their sort anywhere and hundreds of thousands of New Yorkers jammed them every weekend. You won't see crowds like that now—thank goodness! But there's plenty to do to keep a family busy down here all afternoon and as far into the evening as they want to stay.

First of all is the beach. It's busy on summer weekends but not jammed, and weekdays provide all the space you want for spreading your blanket on the sand. The beach is clean and well

It's hard to beat a day at the beach at Coney Island

patrolled, with plenty of lifeguards and public toilets. This is the Atlantic Ocean, remember, so the water is cold in early summer and, well, bracing even in August, but kids are tough. And so are parents. Come on in—the water's fine! Really! (Usually. We've never been tempted to join the annual New Year's Day "Polar Bear Swim." But if you're in New York then, it's an option, I suppose.)

The beach at Coney (or further down the Boardwalk at Brighton Beach or Manhattan Beach) is a great place for a respite from overheated Manhattan concrete in the summer. The temperature is several degrees lower, the water is cool, and there's always a breeze. What a place for splashing and sand castles! There are places to eat nearby where you can get everything from a vegetarian meal to a greasy or sweet snack. If you want a stroll, the Boardwalk stretches for four miles along the ocean, and even if the day is too cool for swimming, you've got lots of other choices.

Two classic amusement parks sit side-by-side along the Coney Island beach between the Boardwalk and Surf Avenue. Maybe they're not the thrill-a-minute places your grandparents would have found there, but they've got some genuine attractions.

The feature at **Astroland** is the *Cyclone*, one of the world's oldest and most famous roller coasters. This 1927 landmark has a first drop of 90 feet (27m) and a top speed of 68 miles per hour (110kph). The current record on this coaster is 2,361 consecutive rides over a span of almost 104 straight hours—a distance

> ***Tip:*** *Individual rides cost $2 to $4 but you can buy a pass for unlimited rides for about $15. Passes are good for specific blocks of time on weekdays: Mon.-Fri. Noon-6 P.M.; Mon.-Thurs. 4-10 P.M.; or Mon.-Thurs. 8 P.M.-Midnight.*

of more than 1,340 miles (2170km). That's a staggering feat, although setting a record like that would have its ups and downs, I imagine.

A tamer, if wetter, ride is the *Water Flume*, sort of like shooting

The Wonder Wheel provides great views of the beach and the ocean

the rapids without the rocks, and the *Astrotower* takes its victims (There's no other way to put it, really) more than 200 feet (61m) above the beach. It must be a great view, but I'll watch from the ground, if you don't mind. There are lots of kiddie rides, too, several arcades with video and target games, a midway, and places where you can buy all sorts of food that's bad for you. What a great place!

Next door at **Deno's Amusement Park** is an equally great assortment of rides. Pride of place here belongs to the famous *Wonder Wheel*, another Coney landmark. The view from the top of the 150-foot-tall Ferris wheel (46m) is stupendous. There are 25 rides at Deno's, including a nice assortment of kiddie rides, plus arcades, midway games, and a McDonald's restaurant. Deno's has fireworks every Friday night at 9 o'clock. Just one thing. Last time we were there, a couple of lights were burned out on the side of the Ferris wheel, making us wonder just what sort of tricks *"Deno's Wonder eel"* might do! [Astroland is at Surf Ave. and W. 10th St., Brooklyn. Open noon-midnight daily. Deno's is on W. 12th St. at Boardwalk, Brooklyn. Open 11 A.M.-midnight. Both parks are open daily from late May through early Sept., with weekend hours for several weeks in late *spring and early autumn. Subway F, Q, N, W: Stillwell Ave-Coney Island]*

You'll find lots of other attractions in the area. Along Surf Avenue look for **Sideshows by the Seashore**, an old-fashioned 10-in-1 show with fire eaters, contortionists, snake charmers, escape artists, and so on. It's even got a tattooed man, but you can see a lot of those for free in New York. The original location of **Nathan's Famous Hot Dogs** still serves what many New Yorkers insist is the best hot dog in the city. There's no shortage of amusement parks to play in, junk shops to browse in, restaurants to eat in. Even the big subway terminus building is a piece of history, almost a hundred years old and part of a 75-acre complex of subway yards and maintenance shops. The **Coney Island Museum** shows the history and many artifacts of the area's halcyon days. A new minor league professional baseball team, the Brooklyn Cyclones provides a fun and inexpensive evening of sports action.

The area looks a little seedy in spots, it's true. It's not what it was years ago. But it is safe... and it's loads of fun.

New York Aquarium

There's something fishy about Coney Island, and it has nothing to do with an occasional flimflam artist trying to separate tourists from their dollars. The New York Aquarium, one of America's leading oceanographic research and display organizations, sits just a moment's walk from the amusement parks and provides hours of amusement itself.

When Coney was at its peak, the aquarium was still in Battery Park in Manhattan. It moved here, a perfect spot next to the ocean, in 1957 and it's been drawing crowds ever since. Probably the most popular attraction is the daily dolphin show. Although come to think of it, the shark tank is extremely popular. How often do you get to look a huge white Beluga shark right in the eye... and teeth... with just a pane of glass between you? (A rather thick one, fortunately.)

And nobody can resist penguins! The enormous windows of the underwater viewing area allow you to watch these Antarctic birds both waddling comically on land and swimming sleekly through their huge tanks, consorting with the nearby sea lions and walruses. The giant sea turtles are always a hit, too. The collection includes more than 350 species of aquatic life. There's even a Touch Tank, the marine equivalent of a petting zoo. *[Surf Ave. and West 8th St., Brooklyn. Subway F, Q: W. 8th St.-Aquarium]*

Along for the Ride

Every family has one member who decides he's so tired that he just can't walk another step—usually in the jetway getting off the plane. Most people, fortunately, have higher fatigue thresholds, but sooner or later everyone will reach that point; the legs just won't move. You're in luck! New York City has some of the best sitting-down sightseeing in the world… and at prices that can't be beat.

The Roosevelt Island Tram

Roosevelt Island sits in the East River between Manhattan and Queens. It's largely residential now, although it has housed medical and military facilities in past years. Problem is, it makes even less sense to own a boat in the city than it does a horse. So if you live on Roosevelt Island and work in Manhattan—well, you see the difficulty.

The New York Transit System tried for years to connect the island to the rest of the city by subway, but was foiled repeatedly by the high cost and technical problems. In desperation, they decided if they couldn't get to the island by going under the river, perhaps going *over* it would be more successful, and in 1976, the most spectacular piece of the city's mass transit system, the country's only commuter cable car, was opened to the public above Queensboro Bridge.

The tram runs from 59th Street in Manhattan to the island, a distance of 3,100 feet (about 1km) in just 4½ minutes at a speed of 16mph (26kph). That doesn't seem very fast, but it makes the trip go much too quickly. The view of the river and the skyline from the tram's peak of 250 feet (76m) isn't as spectacular as some others, but it's memorable, easy, and cheap.

You get great views of Midtown from the Roosevelt Island Tram

The price is a mere $1.50 per ride and outside of rush hour the tram is seldom crowded. More than 100 people can ride at a time, and the tram makes more than 100 trips a day, even on weekends. I predict that one ride won't be enough, but if it is—there's finally a subway station on the island. [*The Manhattan station is at 60th St. and Second Ave., Upper East Side. Subway N, R: Lexington Ave.; 4, 5, 6: 59th St. The tram runs from 6 A.M. until 2 A.M. daily, and until 3:30 A.M. Fri. and Sat.*]

The Staten Island Ferry

A friend told me once that of all the things her family saw and did on its trip to New York—the tall buildings, the bright lights of Broadway, the world-famous landmarks— the hit of the trip for the kids was riding the Staten Island Ferry. I personally wouldn't rank it *that* high, but I'll agree that it's a real treat with an incredible view and the best price you'll find anywhere—it's absolutely free! Fares (except for cars) were eliminated in 1997.

The ferry runs 24 hours a day, making the trip between Manhattan and Staten Island in 25 minutes. During the wee hours, there's just one trip an hour, but there are ferries every 15 minutes during rush hours and every 20 to 30 minutes midday and evenings—50 trips a day during the week, 32 on weekends and holidays.

Even if you're not going to visit any of the attractions on Staten Island, a trip over and back on the ferry is a relaxing and pleasant hour's break from walking, and the view is phenomenal. But if you want a quick field trip, the terminal is adjacent to the Staten Island Institute of Arts and Sciences. [*The Manhattan terminal is at Whitehall St. and South St., Battery Park, Lower Manhattan. Subway 1, 9: South Ferry; 4, 5: Bowling Green; N, R: Whitehall St. The Staten Island terminal on Richmond Terrace is served by the Staten Island Railway and numerous buses.*]

Family Fun

A Simple Bus Ride

So far our inexpensive sightseeing tours have taken you through the air to Roosevelt Island and on the water to Staten Island. This time we'll stay on dry land and ride through the heart of Manhattan—just hop a bus!

Sightseeing buses (at $20 or so per person) cover New York City thoroughly and offer informative and witty commentary. If you're willing to forego the commentary you can see the same sights on a city bus for much, much less money.

You can use your MetroCard or pay the $1.50 fare with exact change (coins only) and pick up a bus anywhere along its route. Bus stops are clearly marked and buses stop every two or three blocks. Hop on any place along the route.

You can pick up a free Manhattan bus map at any subway station. No single bus goes by *all* the attractions an expensive tour bus covers, but almost every Manhattan bus takes you past landmarks everyone will recognize. A few routes are better than others, though.

You can pick up bus M10 anywhere along Central Park West. (We've used it to save walking from one end of the park to the other when we're weary.) At Columbus Circle at the southwest corner of the park, the bus heads down Broadway, through Times Square to Seventh Avenue. It goes down Seventh as far as Madison Square Garden, then loops back north again, following Eighth Avenue back up to Columbus Circle and Central Park. Going south, sit on the left side of the bus for the best views of the park, Times Square, and the Empire State Building.

Bus M20 starts at Columbus Circle and follows the same route south as the M10. It keeps going beyond Madison Square Garden, though, rolling through Chelsea, through Greenwich Village, and past the World Trade Center, almost to Battery Park. At Battery Park City it loops back north past the World Financial Center and eventually back up Eighth Avenue to Columbus Circle. The left side of this bus has the best views, as well.

You can ride the M5 for miles. It starts at 178th Street in Harlem and runs all the way to Houston Street in Greenwich Village. The best part of the route begins near Grant's Tomb at 122nd Street. The bus runs along Riverside Drive overlooking Riverside Park and the Hudson River until it picks up Broadway at 72nd Street. Now the M5 passes Lincoln Center, turns at Central Park South, and makes its way to Fifth Avenue.

The M5 follows Fifth Avenue as it passes St. Patrick's Cathedral, Rockefeller Center, lots of exclusive shopping, the Public Library, the Empire State Building, the Flatiron Building, and much more. In Greenwich Village the route shifts to Avenue of the Americas and the M5 heads back north past Herald Square, Radio City Music Hall, and more, returning to Central Park South before retracing its steps up Broadway and Riverside Drive. Sit on the right side of this bus.

There's much more. The M1 runs along Museum Mile all the way down the east side of Central Park and goes all the way to the tip of Manhattan. The M6 runs from Central Park to Battery Park via Times Square. Just get a map and try it for yourself. The bus is slower than the subway… but you'll see a lot more.

High Tech

No vacation should be *all* museums and parks and tall buildings. Sometimes what you want to do is just play around. You've come to the right place. The attractions in this section are sure to be a hit with some family members.

Sony Wonder Technology Lab
Who knows more than Sony about electronics? At the Technology Labs in the Sony Building, your family video gamers and audiophiles can have the time of their lives. Five hands-on sections let visitors learn about—and then try—the technology that will drive our 21st-century world. In the *Audio* section, learn how sound waves can see inside the human body. Or maybe

you'd like to record your own CD! Learn about special effects in the *Imaging* exhibit, or edit a music video.

You can program a factory in the *Artificial Intelligence* section and design video game graphics or technical products in Sony's *Design* section. The *Networks* exhibit focuses on communication technology and the future. And it's all free. *[550 Madison Ave. at E. 56ᵗʰ St., Midtown. Subway E, F, N, R, W: 5ᵗʰ Ave. Closed Mon. Free]*

Lazer Park

Not a park at all, this big indoor entertainment center in Times Square might be the best of the several arcades in the area. Enter this labyrinthine basement and choose from scores of the newest and hottest video games. Try lifelike virtual reality simulations like car racing or skiing—with everything but the bruises. Or step from the virtual world into the real one and play laser tag, stalking your opponent in a blacklit world of mazes, tall columns, and blinds. *[163 W. 46ᵗʰ St. at Broadway, Midtown. Numerous subway lines serve the Times Square area. Free admission—but the games cost. Open until 2 A.M. (11 P.M. Sun.)]*

New York Skyride

Thrillseekers don't have to go all the way to Coney Island and ride the Cyclone. They can go to the Second Floor of the Empire State Building and take a simulated ride over New York. The seats sway and pitch as passengers hurtle through the air high above the city, plunge into the canyons between skyscrapers, and get phenomenal big-screen views of the skyline that's normally reserved only for birds. But a confession is in order: I haven't actually been on it: I don't have the stomach for it. But kids, still breathing hard on exit, assure me it's great. *[Fifth Ave. at 34ᵗʰ St., Midtown. Subway B, D, F, N, Q, R, W: 34ᵗʰ St. Open until 10 P.M.]*

Sporting Life

While walking in New York City provides all the exercise *I* need, it's nice to be able to get some recreation or even a good workout—or better yet, watch *other* people exercise.

Chelsea Piers

Four unused piers along the Hudson River now house New York's most impressive fitness complex. Some facilities in the 30-acre complex are limited to members who pay extravagant sums, even by New York standards, to join, but others are open to the public on a pay-per-use basis for an amount that won't require getting another mortgage on your house.

I'll give you just a sample of what's available. An indoor driving range, 40-lane bowling alley, basketball courts, two year-round ice rinks, two outdoor roller rinks, gymnastics and swimming classes, two indoor soccer fields, batting cages, martial arts training, dance studios, rock climbing wall, marina, movie theaters, restaurants—oh! I haven't exercised at all and I'm exhausted. They call it a "Sports Village" and it truly is. *[W 24ᵗʰ St. at the Hudson River, Chelsea. Subways are not close but it's easy to take subway 1, 9, C, E to 23ʳᵈ St. and transfer (free) to an M23 bus, which stops at the entrance. Times and prices vary by facility. Check the Chelsea Piers web page for information]*

Midtown Skating

One of the great New York wintertime traditions is ice skating at Rockefeller Plaza. The rink is open daily until after 10 P.M. all winter long—the exact dates will vary according to the weather but late October until the end of March is typical. Of course it costs. Most things do in New York. Count on averaging $10 per person, plus $7 to rent skates if you didn't bring your own. If you like ice skating, though, there's no better place within a hundred miles, especially during the Christmas season, when Rockefeller Center's gigantic Christmas tree looms above the

Ice skating at Rockefeller Plaza is a Manhattan tradition

skaters. *[Fifth Ave. between 49th and 50th streets, Midtown. Subway B, D, F, S: Rockefeller Ctr.]*

The Pros
New Yorkers are huge fans of professional sports. To see just how seriously they take their local teams, attend a game. During the summer you can watch one of the city's two major league baseball teams. The **Yankees** play at Yankee Stadium *[161st St. at River Ave., The Bronx. Subway B, D, 4: 161st St-Yankee Stadium]* and the **Mets** play at Shea Stadium *[Flushing, Queens. Subway 7: Willets Point-Shea Stadium]*.

In the winter you can go to Madison Square Garden *[West 33rd St. and Eighth Ave., Chelsea. Subway A, C, E, 1, 2, 3, 9: Penn Station-34th St.]* to see professional basketball with the **Knicks** or ice hockey with the **Rangers**. The women's pro basketball team, the **Liberty**, also plays here. The sports pages of any daily newspaper will give you the current schedule. New York's professional football teams, however, no longer play in New York. They share a stadium in East Rutherford, New Jersey.

Tennis

One of the world's four Grand Slam tennis tournaments, the U.S. Open, is played in New York. The National Tennis Center in Queens is a state-of-the-art facility, the largest public tennis facility in the world, with 33 outdoor courts and nine indoor courts available to the public. Sorry—the famous tournament courts (Arthur Ashe Stadium and Louis Armstrong Stadium) aren't available to you unless you get very, very good! The National Tennis Center sits between Flushing Meadows-Corona Park and Shea Stadium. *[Flushing, Queens. Subway 7: Willets Point-Shea Stadium]*

Recommendations

✔ Get out of the museum mode occasionally and have some silly fun at the beach, a video arcade, or a skating rink.

✔ Try at least one of the city's special rides: Tram, ferry, or bus.

✔ Big sports fans should check out one of the city's famous professional facilities. Even if the team you want to see is out of town, tours of the stadium or arena are often available.

14. Engaging Entertainment

The first time I ever visited New York City was to speak at a convention, and I had a long list of things I wanted to do while I was in town—see the Statue of Liberty, go up in the Empire State Building... my list probably wasn't very much different from that of any other first-time visitor.

But at the very top of my list was to see a Broadway show. I love theater (My London books devote a lot of space to it) and couldn't wait to go to a show on the world's most famous theater street. I saw not one but two famous musicals—starring famous actors—on that trip, and am seldom in the city now without taking in at least one show, either on Broadway or off.

But Broadway is just the tip of New York's entertainment iceberg. In this chapter I'll tell you what you need to know about taking the family to one of the big-name (and big price tag) shows, but also show you some of the other fun—and cheaper—possibilities. But let's start with the stage.

Playing Around

New Yorkers think their city is the center of creation. Whether it is or not, *Times Square* is the center of New York. Oh, not geographically. That would have to be somewhere in Brooklyn.

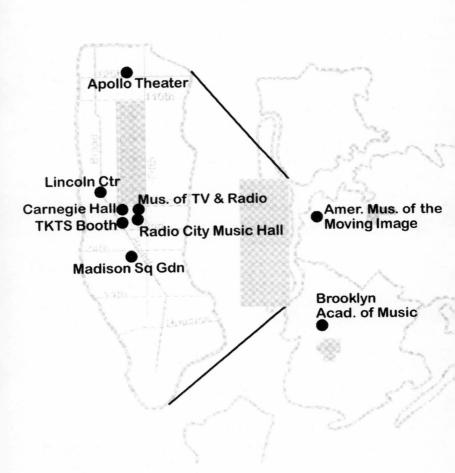

Chapter 14 Highlights

I think. But everyone goes to Times Square on their first visit; nowhere else in this great city is more vibrant.

Times Square is a curiosity. People from all over the country watch the live celebrations here on television every New Year's Eve, and at the stroke of midnight, feel that the new year has begun—even if they're watching in San Francisco, where it's still only 9 o'clock. No telling what you'll encounter here: A guy encased in a huge block of ice, possibly... camera crews from all over the world shooting commercials and news reports or television shows, probably... people of every description hurrying on their separate errands or just gawking, certainly. At 3 o'clock in the morning there are probably more people out in Times Square than lived in the town I grew up in.

And we won't even discuss how many of them are talking on their cell phones.

In the 1970s and 80s, this area had a well-earned reputation for seediness; pornography was its major industry. That's all changed now and aside from one or two unobtrusive peep shows, all the entertainment is so clean it squeaks. Nowhere is the city as well patrolled by the police (there's even a police station in the middle of Broadway) so don't be reluctant to visit.

Broadway Shows

Of course you'll want to take in a show, but whether you do that on this trip will depend on the ages of your kids, on what's playing, and on your budget.

You'll find a few shows, like *Beauty and the Beast* or *The Lion King*, that are great family entertainment, even for the youngest of your clan. If the kids are *too* small, though, avoid taking them to other shows. It will be expensive for you and boring for the little ones. Kids older than 10 or 12 will manage fine with almost anything, although musicals and more elaborate shows will do a better job of keeping them entertained. Avoid serious, dialogue-heavy plays for pre-high schoolers.

New York City for Families

How do you know what's playing and what might be suitable? Times Square is filled with magazine stands along the sidewalk. Any of them can sell you a copy of either *Time Out* or *New York* magazine. These are great guides to the city. Both have listings of what's playing in every theater in town, and include capsule summaries, reviews, showtimes, and prices that will help you choose. When I get to New York I usually buy a copy of each magazine right at the airport, although I find *Time Out* to be more comprehensive (as well as about a dollar cheaper). Major hotels also usually offer free copies of *Where* magazine, which has decent listings. You can also pick up free copies of the *Village Voice*, which has plenty of entertainment listings.

It's easy to find out what's playing. Here's the painful part:

Popular Broadway shows can cost you a hundred dollars a seat.

And anything your family wants to see will probably fall into that *Popular* category.

Times Square is a cacophony of images and color all day long

Some shows will have reduced prices for students, available only at the box office shortly before the performance, but you shouldn't count on this. Don't expect Sunday matinee prices to be lower, either—the discount is usually only a few dollars even when there is one. No, if you want to go to one of the most popular shows, you'll have to pay what it takes. Tickets can be purchased directly at the box office or from the Ticketmaster website (for an additional service charge) listed in the appendix. Remember that popular shows can be sold out weeks or months in advance. Ticket agencies can get you last-minute tickets to almost any show… but at a *huge* markup.

The good news is— there are alternatives! See the sidebar *Cheap(er) Tickets* for your financial salvation.

Cheap(er) Tickets

Remember our walk through Midtown in Chapter 6? As we strolled through Times Square, I pointed out the TKTS booth at 47th Street and Broadway. Now is the time to stop there.

The Theatre Development Fund runs two booths in Manhattan that sell discount seats to Broadway and some other shows. These are tickets that have gone unsold at full price, released by the theaters on the day of the performance to sell at the TKTS booths, at a discount of 25% to 50%. The most popular shows will never be available here because, obviously, if a show is sold out, there aren't any unsold tickets to release. But long-running plays and musicals are always available, and last year's hit might be this year's discount. We always buy our theater tickets here.

This is a great choice for a family that wants to go to a Broadway show but doesn't have a special must-see in mind, because there is always a large assortment of shows available, posted on a signboard in front of the booth. Just join the long line (it moves quickly and there are always musicians or acrobats to entertain you— be sure to give them a dollar or two) and wait your turn.

Have several choices in mind, in case the show you planned to see is sold out when you get to the front of the line. Check the board and make a list, then one person can wait in line and buy the tickets while everyone else does some sightseeing or shopping nearby. (cont.)

No credit cards are accepted: Payment must be in cash or traveler's checks (in U.S. dollars) only. Remember that the tickets you buy are for today only; the Times Square booth does not sell advance tickets.

If you're in Lower Manhattan, you'll also find a TKTS booth on the mezzanine of the World Trade Center, Building 2. The process is exactly the same as in Times Square, with two exceptions. First, the line is shorter. (I didn't say short. It's not. But it's not quite as long... and it's indoors, which is nice if the day is cold or rainy.) Second, this booth sells tickets one day in advance for Saturday and Sunday matinees. So you can get tickets to a Saturday afternoon show on Friday, or a Sunday afternoon performance on Saturday. The Times Square booth doesn't do that.

Prices are the same at both locations— 25% to 50% off face value, plus a small service charge per ticket. [TKTS Booth Times Square: Open Mon.-Sat. 3-8 p.m. and 11 a.m.-2 p.m. Sat. for matinee tickets. Sun. 11 a.m.-7 p.m. TKTS Booth World Trade Center 2: Open Mon.-Fri. 11 a.m.-5:30 p.m., Sat. 11 a.m.-3:30 p.m.]

Off & Off-off Broadway Shows

If you want a New York theater experience and don't want to take a second mortgage on your house to buy enough tickets for the family, you have choices in this city's lively theater scene. I checked as I was writing this chapter (a typical week) and found at that point there were 29 Broadway shows running—but 94 Off Broadway and Off-off Broadway shows available. Theatergoers are truly spoiled for choice!

Off Broadway shows don't offer a lesser theater experience. They may be held in smaller theaters (occasionally, curiously enough, in theaters that are *on* Broadway)—even in churches or other buildings or in parts of the city away from the Theater District—and their tickets cost less... often *much* less. But some of New York's very best entertainment is found Off Broadway, from the unexplainable performance artists *Blue Man Group* to the Pulitzer Prize winning *W;t* (Yes, that's the spelling) to New York's longest-running play *The Fantasticks* (more than 40 years old and showing no sign's of slowing down... unlike most of us over-40s!)

Tickets to some Off Broadway shows even can be obtained from TKTS booths, while others are available only from the box office. Both *Time Out* and *New York* magazines

> ***Tip:*** *If you've visiting in the summer and enjoy Shakespeare, skip ahead to Chapter 16 and read about the Delacorte Theatre's Shakespeare in Central Park performances. They're free!*

provide phone numbers for theaters in their listings. Lots of big-name shows started Off Broadway, and moved uptown when they became hits.

Off-off Broadway shows are usually in smaller venues yet, with even lower ticket prices. You might see plays you're familiar with, but you might also see the work of new playwrights, experimental shows, or other oddities. Before taking your family to a show like this, you might telephone the theater and make sure it's suitable for all the members of your group.

Try one of the smaller playhouses

High Culture

The average 4-year-old might not be overwhelmed by "serious" music, but if family tastes run toward this sort of thing, you can't do much better than New York City. Here are some of the country's leading settings for great music. Check music listings in *Time Out* and you might find some surprises, like great jazz, classic folk, world music from around the globe, or ancient and Renaissance music.

Please don't ask someone on the street how to get to **Carnegie Hall**. The answer will certainly be "Practice, practice, practice!" It's easier than that: All you have to do is buy a ticket to performances by some of the most acclaimed musicians in the world. Even easier, go to the Family Concert Series on Saturday afternoons from October to May for just $5 (Reserve at 212-903-9670). The hall also contains a museum and tours are available. *[154 W. 57th St., Midtown. Subway N, R, Q, W: 57th St.]*

An even more impressive temple of the arts is **Lincoln Center**, a complex of sites on the Upper West Side that is home to the New York Philharmonic, the Metropolitan Opera, the New York City Ballet and a variety of other groups in an assortment of glorious performance spaces. The center offers an enormous variety of programs for young people and backstage tours of the theaters in the complex. *[Broadway and W. 65th St., Upper West Side. Subway 1, 9: 66th St-Lincoln Ctr.]*

Another place less savvy tourists miss because it's not in Manhattan is the **Brooklyn Academy of Music** *[30 Lafayette Ave., Brooklyn. Subway 2, 3, 4, 5, Q: Atlantic Ave.; C: Lafayette Ave.; G: Fulton St.]* BAM, as it's called, is the country's oldest performing arts center, and has a special commitment to world music and to education. Check BAM's website before you arrive and you might have another good reason to flee Manhattan for a day.

Popular Culture

Everyone in the world thinks they know what the United States is like, because the world's television and movie screens are dominated by American programs and films. Of course visitors usually find a different country from the one they expect once they get here (In my, uh, *many* years of life, for instance, I've *never* seen a car chase or a gun battle), but there's no denying the power of the images projected to the rest of the world.

New York has a couple of good places to learn about the images. For example, everyone will see some familiar things at the **American Museum of the Moving Image**. *[35th Ave. at 36th St., Queens. Subway N, W: 36th Ave.]* Housed in Astoria Studio in Queens, one of the country's leading film studios in the silent, pre-Hollywood era, the museum is packed full of TV and film artifacts from Orson Welles' costumes and makeup from *Citizen Kane* and Robin Williams' female bodysuit in *Mrs. Doubtfire* to the complete set of Monks Café, where so many scenes from *Seinfeld* were shot. There are great exhibits on how TV shows and movies are produced, and a variety of films are screened in the museum's theater every day. Kids will enjoy the Magic Mirror that lets them model costumes, and they can create their own 70-frame, 10-second animation.

The **Museum of Television and Radio** *[25 W. 52nd St., Midtown. Subway E, F: Fifth Ave.]* holds a vast archive of TV and radio programs. Some are shown in the public galleries each day, but virtually everything in the collection is at your disposal. All you have to do is register when you arrive, then use the museum's computerized database to find the television or radio program you want. The program is played for you in the museum's console room minutes later.

All most people know about **Radio City Music Hall** is that it's home to the leggy Rockettes. But this mammoth Rockefeller Center theater has one of the world's largest performing stages. Go to a show here if you can. The theater underwent extensive renovation that restored it to its original 1932 splendor. Extensive tours are also available daily until 5 P.M., but they are expensive, more than $50 for a family of four. But it's worth it for the true theater buff. *[1260 Sixth Ave. at 50ᵗʰ St., Midtown. Subway B, D, F, S: 47-50ᵗʰ St.-Rockefeller Ctr.]*

You won't find nearly as much regular TV programming in New York now as was once the case; most of the production has moved to California. But here are a few spur-of-the-moment possibilities. If your family consists of early risers (this would never have worked for the Lains), go to Rockefeller Center between 7 A.M. and 9 A.M. any weekday and watch the popular NBC network morning program *Today* through the windows on East 49ᵗʰ Street. There's a good chance a few million people will see you waving. Afterwards, you can take a tour of the NBC studios.

Fans of the *David Letterman Show* can wander up to the Ed Sullivan Theater at West 53ʳᵈ Street and Broadway. The program tapes there at 5 P.M. Monday through Thursday, and it's not unusual for cameras to make their way into the street or for an "alternate studio audience" to be formed. The music network MTV also has studios in the area, behind the big windows at West 45ᵗʰ Street and Broadway. You'll spot the crowds waving to the cameras shooting through the big windows above Lindy's Restaurant.

Other Venues

Sports events like professional and college basketball and professional ice hockey, plus circuses, ice shows, rodeos, and all kinds of marvelous entertainment—more than 600 events a year—are the fare at **Madison Square Garden** *[West 33ʳᵈ St. and Eighth Ave., Midtown. Subway A, C, E, 1, 2, 3, 9: Penn Station-34ᵗʰ St.]* Ticket prices can be either high or family-friendly, depending on the event, and a behind-the-scenes tour is available here, too, that might take you into a pro basketball locker room or into the center ring of a circus, depending on what's going on that day.

The premier venue for a generation of black entertainers, the **Apollo Theater** *[253 W. 125th St., Harlem. Subway A, B, C, D, 2, 3:125th St.]* hosted some of the finest singers and musicians of the twentieth century when their color kept them from performing further downtown. It's still a place with great entertainment, and is worth paying homage to on a walk through Harlem even if it's not booked with an act you want to see.

This chapter could run on forever. If you're still in the mood for more, the city's entertainment magazines are must reading.

Recommendations

✔ Go to the theater, on, off, or off-off Broadway. It's probably illegal to visit New York and not do so.

✔ TV shows are fun. Take a studio tour or get up early and wave to the cast of the *Today* show.

✔ The American Museum of the Moving Image provides a great excuse to visit Queens. Combine it with other Queens attractions.

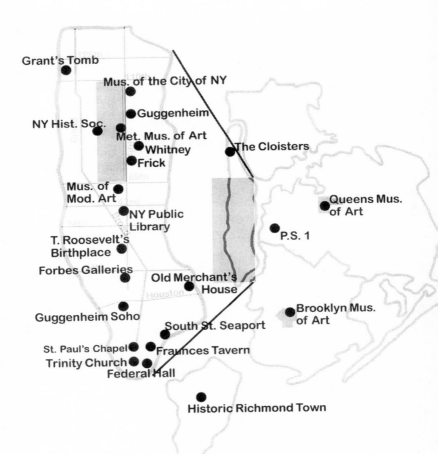

Chapter 15 Highlights

15. Historical Highlights

Istory and art: Two words to make any kid's eyes light up... or perhaps I mean glaze over. I think I know why. Both subjects are too often taught in school as something remote. If history is about the dead past, places and times that have no connection with us, memorized lists of people we don't know about or care about—well, no wonder it bores kids to death! And if art is just European paintings of places we've never been in a style we don't know enough about to see what makes it special, no wonder most kids would rather watch TV.

It doesn't have to be that way. If a child (or an adult, for that matter) can listen to the stories of history, get to know its characters as people pretty much like the rest of us, and see the great varieties of art the world produces... much of it incomprehensible—or just plain silly—to us but special to somebody, then those subjects come alive.

I don't want to suggest that kids will inevitably resist historical and artistic corners of the city; many thrive on it. When I was a child, back when the Earth was still cooling, I was fascinated by history. Of course there was a lot less of it then.

There is apparently something of a voyeur in me. I was never interested in battles and generals and kings, especially, but I *was* interested in ordinary people and how they lived their lives. I was interested in people's stories, and history let me become part of their lives for a little while.

Art was an extension of the same thing. I always looked at paintings (a thing society approves of) like I was sneaking a peek through a window (which society does *not* approve of), spying on part of someone's life. Kinky, perhaps, but it developed an appreciation of both subjects. You can spy a lot of interesting things on this trip.

The Best Places to See History

We've already dabbled in history in earlier chapters. The *Intrepid*, the Fire Museum, the Tenement Museum—all of these served up historical ambiance and information by the ladleful. New York has so many places, though, where you can just wallow in history and connect it to today, that we've got to look at some more closely.

Let's start by ignoring the advice of a New Yorker who told me, "There's no point in going down in the Wall Street area. There's nothing down there anybody but a banker would be interested in." But I like to see for myself, and I'm glad I did.

Early America
If I'd followed the advice of my friend, I would have missed standing on the spot where George Washington took the oath of office that made him the first president of the United States. **Federal Hall** is actually a relatively new building, begun in 1834. The really historic things took place in its predecessor. But it's a marvelous old building, very different from the modern skyscrapers that surround it.

In the original building on this site in 1735, newspaper publisher John Peter Zenger was tried by the British crown for printing articles protesting the actions of the royal governor.

George Washington became the country's first president on the site where Federal Hall now stands

Zenger's acquittal helped set the stage for America's free press. On this site, New York's colonial government called a special meeting in 1765 to protest the taxes known as the Stamp Act— protests which helped lead to the American Revolution ten years later. On this site in 1775, George Washington addressed the Provincial Congress about his dreams of a democracy in America if the Revolution, underway for just a few months, should be won. And on this site in 1789, Washington became the first leader of that democracy.

The building is now part of the National Park Service and contains many exhibits illustrating the history of this part of New York. [*26 Wall St., Lower Manhattan. Subway 2, 3, 4, 5: Wall St.; 1, 9, N, R: Rector St. Free*]

From the sidewalk in front of Federal Hall, peer all the way up the street to your right. Looking very much out of place framed by modern skyscrapers is **Trinity Church**, one of the most historic churches in the city. The present church was opened in 1846, when it was the tallest building in the city, but

Historic Trinity Church stands at the head of Wall Street

there have been two previous churches on the site, dating back to 1697, when the parish was established by the Anglican Church of England. The notorious pirate Captain William Kidd was a member of that first congregation.

King William III granted the charter to that first church, and rented it the land for the nominal payment of one peppercorn per year. Even that modest rent was never paid, but when the church was visited by Queen Elizabeth II on a trip to America in 1976, the parish presented her with 279 peppercorns in back rent.

Entering the present church, you will undoubted be drawn to the marvelous stained glass window behind the high altar, some of the oldest stained glass in the United States. Walk through the graveyard and you'll find the graves of the American patriot Alexander Hamilton and the inventor of the steamboat, Robert Fulton. *[Wall St. at Broadway, Lower Manhattan. Subway 2, 3, 4, 5: Wall St.; 1, 9, N, R: Rector St. Free]*

From the front of the church, turn left and take a ten-minute stroll north to **St. Paul's Chapel**. Founded in 1766 as a branch of Trinity Church, this is a wonderful, historic old building, the last remaining colonial church in New York City. George Washington attended services here the day he was inaugurated president in 1789, and the pew he used is carefully preserved, along with the first painting even made of the Great Seal of the United States, which hangs behind the pew. *[Broadway at Fulton St., Lower Manhattan. Subway N, R: Cortland St.; A, C: Broadway-Nassau; 2, 3, 4, 5, J, M, Z: Fulton St. Free]*

Living History

Preserved or restored slices of the everyday life of the past—these have always been Lain family favorites, and New York City offers many places where you can see how New Yorkers of old lived their lives. As long as we're in Lower Manhattan anyway, let's start with a couple of spots in the same area.

The **Fraunces Tavern** is where President Washington said goodbye to the officers who had served under him during the American Revolution in his famous "Farewell Address" in 1783. The building later housed several governmental offices and, since a thorough restoration in 1907 has had an excellent museum of the period. *[54 Pearl St., Lower Manhattan. Subway 4, 5: Bowling Green; J, M, Z: Broad St.]*

Every American president has had a connection to the city

One of Lower Manhattan's neatest places is the **South Street Seaport**. This area of several square blocks is worth a morning of your time if your group has any interest in history or seafaring. This marvelous collection of museums, shops, and restaurants vividly portrays the area's history. From the lighthouse at Pearl Street (a monument to the *Titanic*), to the authentic old sailing ships moored in the river, this is a vibrant, evocative area.

Climb aboard the tall, four-masted *Peking*, built in 1911 and a veteran of voyages to South America and Africa. Watch the ongoing restoration of the 325-foot-long (100m) *Wavertree*, the largest remaining sailing ship built of iron. Visit a tugboat pilot house, a nineteenth-century printshop, a gallery of model ships and ocean liner memorabilia, a fine children's center with workshops and exhibits, the Maritime Crafts Center, a boat-building shop, and much more.

Old sailing ships are one of the many attractions at South Street Seaport

Pick up a map and information about the attractions from the visitor center on Fulton Street, then slip back into the nineteenth-century. If some family members would rather shop, Pier 17 has three floors of places to browse and buy. Later you can all meet for lunch at the end of the pier with a spectacular view of the Brooklyn Bridge. This should be on almost any family's "must-do" list. [Water St. to the East River between John and Beekman streets, Lower Manhattan. Subway 2, 3, 4, 5, J, M, Z: Fulton St. Prices and times of attractions vary.]

Tip: For a genuine taste—and smell!—of the sea, wander through the adjacent Fulton Fish Market. Mornings are the time to go here, since the market sells the daily catch to restaurants and markets all over the city and the stalls are empty and shut by midday.

A couple of miles north of here, in the East Village, is the **Old Merchant's House**, a residence built in 1831 which preserves much of its original furnishings and fixtures, giving a good look at the way the growing upper middle class lived in the New York of two centuries ago. [29 E. 4th St., East Village. Subway 6: Bleecker St.; F, S: Broadway-Lafayette St. Closed Fri. and Sat. Open 1–4 P.M. only]

A fine local historical site is found in the heart of Staten Island, and so is seldom visited by tourists. It's **Historic Richmond Town**, a 100-acre complex of buildings set up as a village containing slices of island life from the seventeenth to the twentieth centuries with large doses of Staten Island history. [441 Clark Ave., Staten Island. Bus S74 from the ferry terminal. Closed Mon. and Tues. as well as weekends Jan. to Mar. Open afternoons only except during the summer]

Museum Pieces

If a little visiting has made you a real junkie for information about New York, you have some nice choices to feed your habit.

Presidential Places

Everyone has heard the whimsical question "Who's buried in Grant's Tomb?" The answer is at the end of this sidebar.

*Every American president has visited New York at one time or another but some have a more intimate connection with it than others. Two historical stopovers might be fun. One is the **Birthplace of Theodore Roosevelt** [28 E. 20th St. Chelsea. Subway N, R: 23rd St. Closed Mon. and Tues. Children free] Roosevelt lived here from 1858 to 1872. The original house was torn down in 1916 but rebuilt a few years later to honor the president.*

Ulysses S. Grant was the North's most famous Civil War general, and served as president of the re-United States from 1869 to 1877. His tomb deteriorated badly over the years, but was restored in 1997. It sits on Riverside Drive at 122nd Street. [Subway 1, 9: 116th St.]

And no one is buried there. President and Mrs. Grant are entombed there, but their bodies are above ground, not below, so technically they are not buried at all!

The best is probably the **Museum of the City of New York** along Museum Mile on the Upper East Side. Here you can see how the city grew from a little Dutch village to its present status as the most important city in the world, discover how New Yorkers of bygone years lived and worked and dressed, even learn about the history of American theater. The museum also sponsors fascinating temporary exhibitions. Recent ones have included a gallery of more than 10,000 toys from the 1700s to the present, music in New York, the history of baseball, and circuses of the city. Whenever you visit, you're bound to find something that will please. [1220 Fifth Ave. at E. 103rd St., Upper East Side. Subway 6: 103rd St. Closed Mon. and Tues. Donation requested]

Across the park is the oldest museum in the city, the **New York Historical Society**. Kids might be less interested in these exhibits than those in some other places, but there are collections of Tiffany lamps, tools, and toys. [W. 77th St. at Central Park West, Upper West Side. Subway B, C: 81st St. Closed Mon. Donation requested]

You'll even find exhibits of more than just books at the **New York Public Library**—exhibitions include art and historical pieces, and the building itself is worth a visit. If nothing else, you'll want to stop and pet the famous lions, Patience and Fortitude, who have guarded the entrance since 1911. [*Fifth Ave. at 42ⁿᵈ St., Midtown. Subway 7, B, D, F, S: 42ⁿᵈ St. Closed Sun., open until 9 P.M. Mon. and Wed. Free*]

The Best Places to See Art

I have to warn you—I'm not going to spend nearly enough time on this section. There's too much to talk about, *way* too much to see in a few days... or a few years. You'll certainly want to visit at least one art museum. Let the kids decide which one. If votes are divided, maybe it would be a good day for the family to split into smaller groups, and compare notes at dinner later. Or, if you're lucky, they'll want to go to more than one.

The Metropolitan Museum of Art
We *must* begin with "The Met," as locals refer to it. This is one of the largest and most distinguished art museums in the world and an almost automatic choice for every visitor with the slightest interest in art or history. Everything is here: prehistoric art, Egyptian artifacts; Greek and Roman art; suits of armor, weapons, and medieval art; enough famous Old Masters and Impressionists to fill a textbook with familiar images; sculpture; weird, wonderful, and perplexing modern pieces; religious art; Asian art; Islamic and Middle Eastern art; musical instruments; centuries of clothing and costumes... Where do I stop?

If it's mummies and Egyptian artifacts you want, stay on the first floor (Europeans—that's the ground floor), turn right from the main entrance and go all the way to the end of the building. The entire northeast corner contains galleries of Egyptian art. The Arms and Armor collection is just beyond the last of the Egyptian galleries. European painting, the Oriental collections, and American art are upstairs.

Printed information and audio guides are available in English, French, German, Italian, Japanese, and Spanish, and printed information only in a few other languages. *[Fifth Ave. at E. 82nd St., Upper East Side. Subway 4, 5, 6: 86th St. Closed Mon. Open until 9 p.m. Fri. and Sat. Under 12 free]*

The Met also has a wonderful separate museum devoted exclusively to medieval art, and it is one of my favorite places in the entire city. **The Cloisters** is located at the far northern end of Manhattan, but it's worth the trip if anybody wants to get the feel of what things were like a thousand years ago. In fact, the building alone is worth the trip. Even though it was built in the 1930s (by John D. Rockefeller, Jr.), it has the look and feel of something many centuries older. You feel like you're in another world here, looking out over the park and the Hudson River. In fact, Rockefeller even bought hundreds of acres of New Jersey land across the river to prevent its development and to retain the peaceful view and atmosphere of the museum.

The collection is wonderful, consisting of everything from tiny individual art objects and artifacts to entire rooms and chapels brought over piece by piece from Europe. Don't miss the Unicorn Tapestries, woven in Belgium more than 500 years ago, the Fuentidueña Chapel, donated by the Spanish government from an ancient church in northern Spain, the chapter house from a medieval French monastery, and the lovely, peaceful outdoor cloisters, perhaps the most serene places in the city. It's an educational and evocative spot. *[In Fort Tryon Park at Riverside Dr. Subway A: 190th St. Closed Mon. Under 12 free]*

Modern Masterpieces

Some people love the feeling of antiquity they experience at the Met and the Cloisters, and others prefer the challenging (and sometimes bewildering) world of modern art. If that's your preference, New York has a couple of great places for you to choose from.

In Chapter 10 you heard about the architectural wonder of the **Guggenheim Museum** *[1071 Fifth Ave. at E. 89ᵗʰ St., Upper East Side. Subway 4, 5, 6: 86ᵗʰ St. Closed Thurs. Open until 8 P.M. Fri. and Sat. Under 12 free].* The Guggenheim is more than just a pretty face. The collection focuses on work of the twentieth century and includes the cubism of Picasso, the pop art of Andy Warhol, the

Visitors almost always overlook the Brooklyn Museum of Art, one of the country's oldest and best

abstract expressionism and non-objective painting of numerous artists. Kids often enjoy this sort of art. And the presentation is unrivaled in the art world. There's no going from gallery to gallery in a rabbit warren of rooms. You simply ascend the spiral ramp from ground to brilliant glass dome, an art experience like no other. If you're in the neighborhood, the **Guggenheim Museum Soho** *[575 Broadway, Soho. Subway N, R: Prince St. Closed Tues. and Wed. Free]* is worth a stop. There's more modern art here, with a special emphasis on multimedia, electronic, and computer-generated art.

Post-Impressionist paintings, like van Gogh's *The Starry Night* are the big draw at the **Museum of Modern Art.** *[11 W. 53ʳᵈ St., Midtown. Subway E, F: 5ᵗʰ Ave. Closed Wed. Open until 8:15 P.M. Fri. Under 16 free. 4:30–8:15 Fri.: pay what you wish]* There is so much more in this, the world's largest collection of modern painting. In fact, kids will probably prefer the Design collection, which

Art Beyond Manhattan

If you insist, like most tourists, on remaining in Manhattan, you're going to miss a lot of cool stuff. You've been warned.

How can you be one of the ten largest museums in the country and be almost unknown to visitors? That's the problem facing the **Brooklyn Museum of Art** [200 Eastern Pkwy, Brooklyn. Subway 2, 3: Eastern Pkwy-Brooklyn Museum. Closed Mon. and Tues. Open until 11 P.M. the first Sat. of the month. Under 12 free]. Its magnificent five-story, nineteenth-century building holds a collection of well over a million objects, one of the most comprehensive art compilations anywhere. The Egyptian collection (3rd floor) is one of the finest in the world, and the coffins (including one for a bird) and mummy cases are usually most popular with kids. The collections of American painting and sculpture are among the best anywhere, especially the watercolors. Collections of Islamic, African, and Asian art and artifacts will fascinate everybody.

If there's an art museum in New York City that is more overlooked than the Brooklyn Museum of Art, it would have to be the **Queens Museum of Art** [Flushing Meadows-Corona Park, Queens. Subway 7: Willets Point-Shea Stadium and follow the signs through the park, about 15 minutes' walk. Closed Mon.] *Founded only in 1972, it is housed in the last remaining building from the 1939 and 1964 World's Fairs in Corona Park. The museum's focus is on twentieth-century art, especially that of the diverse ethnic groups that make up much of Queens, and it plays an important role in arts programming in the borough. But what really brings people into the museum is the spectacular panorama of the city of New York, the world's largest architectural scale model. This is an accurate, detailed three-dimensional model of the entire city and includes a replica of almost every structure in New York. It's kept carefully up to date and alone is worth the modest price of admission.*

As long as we're in Queens, let's stop in at **P.S.1** [22–25 Jackson Ave, Queens. Subway G: 21st St; 7: 45th Rd.; E, F: 23rd St-Ely Ave. Closed Mon. and Tues.], *once a public school and now an innovative contemporary arts center. This is not just exhibition space, but a comprehensive program that provides education and workshops for all ages, and even studio space for artists from all over the world. Many exhibits here are things kids can really get into, like "sound art" or "childhood and contemporary art."*

includes everything from kitchenware and posters to skyscrapers, sports cars, and an inflatable table. It's surely the only *art* museum in the world whose collection includes a helicopter! Older students might like to learn about the film and photograph archives, but for most family members the attraction will be the unexpected, the unusual, and the whimsical.

And Don't Forget…
No one would expect to find prime exhibition space in the lobby of a financial magazine's publishing headquarters. But it's one of the neatest art spots in the city. The **Forbes Magazine Galleries** *[60 Fifth Ave. at 12th St., Greenwich Village. Subway 4, 5, 6, L, N, R: 14thSt-Union Sq. Closed Sun., Mon., and Thurs. Free]* include thousands of toy soldiers, hundreds of toy boats, a dozen Faberge Easter eggs, presidential papers, historical documents, and more.

If you're going to overdose on art, there's also the **Whitney Museum of American Art** *[945 Madison Ave. at E. 75th St., Upper East Side. Subway 6: 77th St. Closed Mon. Open Fri. until 9. Under 12 free. Pay what you wish Fri. 6–9 P.M.]* and the **Frick Collection** *[1 E. 70th St. at Fifth Ave., Upper East Side. Subway 6: 68th St. Closed Mon. Under age 10 not admitted]*

Recommendations

✔ Take in at least one historical and one artistic site. Seeing things first hand is nothing at all like reading about them or seeing pictures in a book.

✔ Unless someone in the family is a serious art student, don't visit more than one art museum per day. They'll blur together in your mind and diminish each other.

✔ Suggest that the kids read something about George Washington or colonial times before the trip to make the historical stops

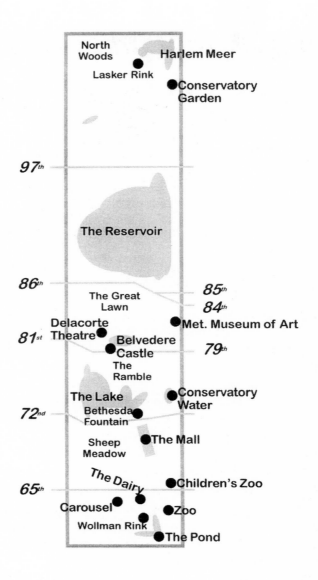

Chapter 16 Highlights

16. Central Park: Cool Place!

I've never devoted an entire chapter to just a single attraction before, but then Central Park is much more than a single attraction—it's a full day's adventure! It doesn't matter if your youngest family member is just 2 years old and the great grandmother you brought along is 88. Everyone will enjoy a day in the park.

Winter and summer, you'll have a great time in Central Park. Even if you're staying in the city only a few days, spend a half day here. If it's a broiling August day, the park is the coolest non-air-conditioned place in Manhattan. On a windy February afternoon you'll get whatever warmth the sun can provide and avoid the wind tunnels created by midtown skyscrapers.

Whether you prefer leafy groves, wide lawns, rugged trails, boating, skating, horseback riding, playgrounds, eating, neat buildings, animal watching, people watching—or just snoozing under a tree while the kids do all those things, Central Park is unmatched for doing them in New York City.

What visitors find most amazing is that every inch of the park was meticulously landscaped. Even the places that look like rugged natural terrain were carefully planned and built, either as part of the park's original 1858 design or in later additions.

Central Park Basics

Central Park is one of the largest urban green spaces in the world, and the most famous one. The park runs for about 2½ miles (4km) through the middle of Manhattan between 59th and 110th streets, and is about a half mile (.8km) wide, laying between 5th and 8th avenues.

Getting to the park is easy. Subway lines 2, 3, A, B, C, D, N, R, Q, and W have stops adjacent to the park. Fifteen Manhattan bus routes run beside or through the park. Anyway, the park is near some of the attractions you will most want to visit. You have no excuse for not going!

Central Park is open until 1 A.M., although no one recommends that you wander alone in remote areas of the park at that hour. But the park is safe, clean, and well patrolled by police—and well populated by visitors from dawn until well past dusk. You'll find plenty of drinking fountains, clean public toilets and lots of places to eat, although it's cheaper and more fun to bring a picnic. Barbecuing and alcoholic beverages are not permitted, however.

If someone in your family likes to walk, run, skate, bike, or just generally move about, Central Park is the place to come to do it safely. Here are miles of trails and roadways. Better yet, cars are banned from park roads (except for a few busy cross streets) all weekend long (6 P.M. Friday until 6 A.M. Monday) and on weekdays from 10 A.M. to 3 P.M. and between 7 and 10 P.M. The Drive, the road that loops around the perimeter of the park, is 6.1 miles (9.8km) around. Walking and cycling maps, and a map of the park, are available free at an information kiosk at East 59th Street and 5th Avenue, and in other places throughout the park.

Because the attractions of the park are so varied, let's just split it into three sections and hit the highlights of each.

The South End (59ᵗʰ to 65ᵗʰ Streets)

Since visitors usually approach the park from the south, this is where most of them spend their time. Even in this six-block area, just a fraction of the park, you can exhaust yourself before you exhaust the attractions. There's enough to do here to weary even the most rambunctious kid. As for the parents, the less said the better....

Near the entrance at 59ᵗʰ Street and 5ᵗʰ Avenue, across the street from the Plaza Hotel, you'll usually find two crowds—horses and artists. They are not, so far as I know, connected in any way. They just both ended up here. The horses, sometimes 20 or 30 of them, are attached to carriages, and their drivers will no doubt ask if you'd like a carriage ride through the park. It can be fun, although the romance of the ride as you imagined it from seeing it in countless movies might be diminished somewhat by the presence of the entire family. It can also be expensive, at almost $40 for a 20-minute ride. That seems short, but it's about all it takes for the novelty to wear off for the kids.

Carriage rides through Central Park are an old, and expensive, New York institution

The artists are on the pavement near the horses, not a place I'd have chosen myself. Here you can buy an original watercolor or pastel, usually of a park scene or some variation on the Manhattan skyline. Or you can have a quick charcoal portrait done. None of these artists is ever likely to have his or her own gallery in the Met up the street, but many are art students and are quite good. If you can find something you like, it can be a neat souvenir of the trip. Buy it at the end of the day, however, not on your way into the park—it's not a fun thing to carry around all day.

If you've been bustling around Manhattan and are all hot and sweaty, you might want to pause near **The Pond** and nature preserve, just inside this entrance on your left, a quiet, shady spot that was enlarged and improved in 2000. But some of the kids might want to head for the zoo instead.

The **Central Park Wildlife Center** is a delightful small zoo that's open until late afternoon every day of the year. Animals are grouped according to the climate of their usual habitats and there's no doubt that the most popular attractions are on the

You can relax by The Pond in Central Park, or just enjoy the view from a stroll along Central Park South

north side of the zoo (on the right when you enter). That's where you'll find the polar bears and penguins. Of course you're apt to get waylaid by the antics of the sea

> ***Tip:*** *If you time your arrival right, everyone will have fun watching the animals eat. The best bets are the sea lions (11:30 A.M., 2 and 4 A.M.) and the penguins (10:30 A.M., 2:30 P.M.).*

lions in the central pool before you can get over there!

After you leave the zoo, continue up the walk (under 65th Street) and pause at the Delacorte Musical Clock and watch the mechanical zoo animals parade to the music every half hour between 8 A.M. and 6 P.M. Just beyond the clock is the **Tisch Children's Zoo**. If you've been in the main zoo, there's no additional charge for admission. Small children will enjoy meeting the baby animals and petting them. The usual suspects—lambs, calves, bunnies, piglets, etc.—are all here.

Make your way back along the south side of 65th Street to **The Dairy**. When it was built in 1870 it really *was* a working dairy, set up to provide fresh milk to local children during a time when much of the city's milk was adulterated and impure. Now the building is a visitor center, chock full of information about the park. The Dairy is the heart of the so-called "Children's District" of the park. For a quiet (well, not necessarily) hour go up to the **Chess and Checkers House** and borrow a board game or some giant chess pieces and have a family tournament. In the wintertime there are few better places for ice skating than **Wollman Rink**. It's larger and less crowded than the one at Rockefeller Center. And the music's louder.

Cross west under the Central Drive through Playmates Arch and go to the **Carousel**. This wonderful hundred-year-old merry-go-round runs in all weather in a building that shelters the carousel and riders—but not the parents who watch their kids whiz around the ride, which costs about $1. When it was built, the Carousel was turned by real horses, but only the wooden ones are left today.

Heart of the Park (65th to 79th Streets)

Cross to the north side of 65th Street and you're looking at a wide, lush expanse of grass, the Sheep Meadow, and beyond it croquet and lawn bowling courts. But bear to the right, toward the long, straight row of trees. This is the **Mall**, the prettiest promenade in Manhattan. At the south end of the walk are statues of literary figures and your family intellectuals can stroll amidst the likenesses of Shakespeare, Robert Burns, Sir Walter Scott, and others. What Columbus is doing with these literary types baffles me.

The mall is lined with tall trees, benches, and food vendors, making it a good place to stop for a cold drink or ice cream cone on a warm day, or perhaps some hot chocolate if it's cold. Near the north end of the mall your family musicians can find statues of Beethoven, Victor Herbert, and other musical bric-a-brac, including a bandshell that's a great place to be on many summer evenings. A short walk east of the bandshell across Rumsey

Playfield there's a statue of Mother Goose—also not exactly in keeping with the theme of the area. That's one of the fun things about Central Park—so carefully planned, but with surprises everywhere.

Rumsey Playfield isn't just for frolicking. Since 1986, it's been home to a marvelous summer series of free entertainment, **Central Park Summer Stage**.

On a clear day, the Lake in Central Park is in a reflective mood

Central Park: Cool Place!

During June, July, and August, SummerStage offers up a dizzying variety of entertainment. One recent summer program consisted of 37 separate events, including world-famous rock bands, grand opera, poetry readings, stilt dancers, Irish dancers, African dancers, jazz and blues artists, brass bands, rappers and hip-hoppers, percussion groups, and the music of Mexico, the Caribbean, South America, North Africa, Israel, Nigeria, Tibet, South Africa, and some that just defies categorizing. Brochures are available in any information booth in the park. Remember—except for one or two benefit shows a summer, it's all *free!*

One of the nicest of the park's visual surprises is yet to come. Continue to the very end of the Mall, across the street, and have your camera ready. You have a fabulous view here of **Bethesda Fountain** and the **Lake**. The only thing marring this wonderful picture is the fact that there is far too often a hot dog vendor on the terrace in front of the fountain. I long to get a photo without having to work my way around the wiener wagon.

It's impossible to pass pretty Bethesda Fountain without taking a picture

Where to go from here? You have many choices. But if you go back across the street and down the steps you can use the public facilities under the street. The walkway under Terrace Drive is worth seeing. Pay attention to the fanciful stonework and trompe l'oeil painting. The effect is something like the undercroft of a medieval monastery.

If you'd like to rent a boat and go rowing or paddling on the lake, the boathouse is a short walk along the shore to your right. If you'd rather sail a miniature boat, walk to the boathouse, cross the road on your right, and follow the path to the **Conservatory Water**, a delightful formal pond. At the boathouse east of the pond you can rent a radio controlled boat for a fun hour of testing your nautical skills. If you come on any Saturday except in the winter, you can watch the highly competitive model boat races. Anyone in your group who has loved the classic E.B. White novel *Stuart Little* will be sure to look for miniature mouse sailors here, because this is the "Sailboat Pond" where Stuart won his big race.

If being Captain Hook isn't anybody's aspiration, cross the lake at Bow Bridge (being sure to stop and take more pictures) and take an amble through the **Ramble**, a maze of trails through the wooded hills north of the lake. Everybody will get a workout

Sail a miniature boat on the Conservatory Water

here, but the paths won't be too challenging for anybody except that 88-year-old great grandmother. Once among the trees, you won't believe you're in the middle of Manhattan.

There are plenty of different routes to follow, but eventually most will come out on a path that leads up a steep hill to the Central Park weather station. And here is another of Central Park's treats.

Belvedere Castle is a whimsical piece of 1872 architecture that presents one of the most dramatic views in New York—or two views, actually. Seen from below near the Turtle Pond, the castle looks as dramatic as its name, perched on rocks above the water, stretching high above the park... although it's not really as big as it appears. From the roof of the

Tip: If short legs (or—sigh!—aging ones) weary of all the walking, you can get from place to place quickly on the bus. If you're headed north, the M10 bus travels along Central Park West. If you're southbound, the M1, M2, M3, and M4 buses run down Fifth Avenue. A weekly MetroCard makes it easy to hop on and off the bus at will. Buses run every 5 to 10 minutes during the day, every 10 to 15 minutes in the evening.

castle, though, you've got a stunning view of the park and uptown. By this time, you'll have to put another roll of film in your camera.

No dungeons inside this castle, though. Instead, the kids will enjoy the wonderful nature discovery center. There's a focus on the birds of the park and the ecology of the area, and exhibits of all sorts of natural objects. Children can use the magnifying glasses, binoculars, telescopes, and microscopes provided, and can borrow a Discovery Kit from the desk, containing a variety of maps, guides to park flora and fauna, and activities. It's a fun and refreshing stop, and one that's surprisingly unmarred by commerce.

It's not actually in Central Park, but just outside the gate at 77th Street and Central Park West (8th Avenue): the American Museum of Natural History. We focused on this museum in Chapter 12, but wanted to remind you about it again, as long as we were in the neighborhood.

The North End (79ᵗʰ to 110ᵗʰ Streets)

We still have half the park to go! We'd better get a move on. Central Park still has wonders galore, but the farther north we go, the fewer visitors we'll find. This is more the natural habitat of the native New Yorker.

You certainly climbed to the roof of Belevedere Castle. As you looked below, just north, you spotted the seats of a large outdoor theater. That's our next stop.

New York is famous for its Broadway theaters, but you can easily pay $100 a ticket to see a show. What most visitors don't realize is that during the summer, one of the best shows in town is free!

The **Delacorte Theatre** presents Shakespeare in Central Park six evenings a week (no performances on Monday) from mid-June through early September. Tickets are distributed free from the theater box office each afternoon beginning at 1 P.M. for that night's show. You can't reserve in advance, but just stop by on your ramble through the park and pick up your tickets. At least half your group will have to stop at the box office, because they'll give you no more than two tickets per person. But you can't beat the price, and you just *can't* have a better day than one spent romping through the park, ending with watching a Shakespeare play under the stars on a warm Manhattan evening.

Just south of the theater is a Shakespeare Garden, where you can find most of the plants mentioned in Shakespeare's plays, and the **Swedish Cottage Marionette Theatre**, home to some of the city's best puppet shows. This is a treat that will please the youngsters in your family—and we oldsters think marionettes are pretty cool, too. Stop by the theater for show times and reservations. Shows are very popular and sell out quickly.

Let's pause again to remind you of another museum. This one

is actually in the park but it's covered in Chapter 15. Of course it's the Metropolitan Museum of Art, one of the great museums of the world. The Met is set into the park along Fifth Avenue between 80th and 84th streets. You won't want to miss it, and this is just a gentle nudge so you don't forget.

Behind the Met is the **Obelisk**, sometimes (just like the similar one in London) called Cleopatra's Needle. This 3,500-year-old structure was a gift from Egypt to the United States and has stood in the park since 1880. It has no known connection with Cleopatra, and in fact was about 1,400 years old before she was even born. This 69-foot (21m) high monolith was in marvelous condition when it came to New York, but the hieroglyphics are nearly worn down now, victim of the kind of weather it never experienced in the desert, and of urban air pollution.

In the center of the park, just west of the Obelisk, is the Great Lawn. Schoolboys used to have to bring permission slips from their principals to be allowed to play baseball here. Now permits from the park office are required. But it's a huge, beautiful lawn. And the best thing about it is that *you* don't have to mow it.

As you walk north you pass playgrounds, paths, and sports facilities everywhere you go. You'll eventually get to the park police station at 85th Street (Central Park has its own precinct), and just beyond, will come to the **Reservoir**.

Once an important part of the city's water system, the Reservoir is now more decorative than functional, and there have even been proposals to fill it in. That's unlikely and it will probably eventually be given over to recreational boating. The paths around the Reservoir are some of the city's most popular jogging and horseback riding spots.

North of the reservoir are many more acres of athletic fields, baseball diamonds, and paths, but if you're looking for a quiet place to sit, walk up the east side of the park to the formal **Conservatory Garden**. This is one of the prettiest and most peaceful spots in Manhattan—even vendors' food carts are forbidden. If you started at 59th Street, you might be ready for a shaded bench by the time you get here, maybe even a 5-minute nap. Your kids might not let you get away with that, but remind them of the signs you'll see asking visitors not to disrupt the peace of the surroundings.

Just past Conservatory Garden is the park's last pond, **Harlem Meer**. This is another pretty, wandering pond, home to countless ducks and geese. (In fact, the island near the west end of the Meer is **Duck Island**.) You must stop at the **Charles A. Dana Discovery Center** on the north side of the Meer: It's one of the best places in Manhattan for your family to learn about nature. The staff presents workshops on a wide variety of topics, sponsors kids' activities like bug hunts, conducts nature walks of the area—even sponsors free evening music and dance events on the plaza beside the pond.

Best of all, there's fishing. At the Discovery Center everyone in your family can borrow a pole and fish in the pond. The Center provides all you need—pole, barbless hooks, even bait. The Meer is stocked with largemouth bass, bluegill, perch, carp, pickerel, shiners, and other species of fish. It's strictly catch-and-release, so you won't have to worry about how to pack your fish when you take it home on the plane. Phew! Fishing is available 11 A.M. to 4:30 P.M. every day but Monday. Behind the Meer, **Lasker Rink and Pool** offer more conventional seasonal fun.

If anyone *still* has energy to burn, they can clamber up the hills in the northwest corner of the park. These are the Cliffs, the Great Hill, and the North Woods—all with a wilderness feel to them. **Blockhouse No. 1**, an old fortification from the War of 1812 is at the top of the Cliffs.

Visitors who go to big cities feel compelled to do traditional "city" things—go to famous museums, shop the famous streets, gawk at famous buildings. There's not a thing wrong with that—that's why you came. But, especially for a family, an occasional change of pace is a must to keep the sense of wonder that brought you to the city in the first place. A person who has been cooped up for too long inside too many museums *will* become a crabby person. It might be the youngest child... but it might be Dad! Spend a day in Central Park. It's one day everybody is guaranteed to enjoy.

Recommendations

✔ Spend at least a half day in Central Park. It will recharge everybody's batteries.

✔ Pick up brochures about events—plays, concerts, walks, etc.—at any park information booth.

✔ Visit one or more of the park's nature centers at the zoo, Belvedere Castle, or the Dana Discovery Center.

✔ Spend a fabulous hour model boating, rowboating, or fishing.

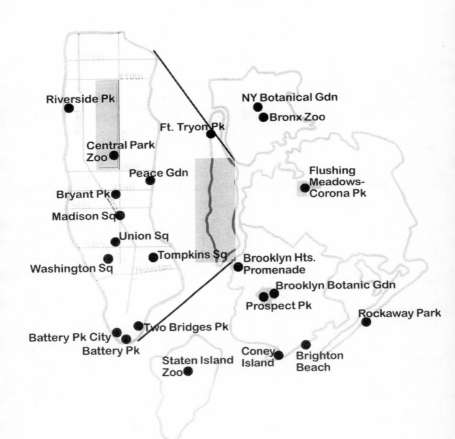

Chapter 17 Highlights

17. Parks and Promenades

A sk the kids to start making a list of the associations that come to mind when you say "New York City." They'll name tall buildings, famous statues and monuments, popular museums, maybe a professional sports team—but they probably *won't* mention any green space except, perhaps, Central Park.

Visitors usually envision New York as an endless sea of concrete and are nearly always surprised to see how green the city is. While, aside from Central Park, it doesn't have huge grass islands in the middle of things like London, New York City has more than its share of pastoral getaway places right in the city. Wherever you're staying… or passing through… in the city, you'll have no trouble finding a leafy place to take off your shoes and relax awhile, or to make your destination for a Sunday picnic.

In this chapter, we'll look at pieces large and small of the city's rural side, some worth making a special trip to see and others ideal for just stopping in as you pass. You'll find your own favorite retreats, too, but these will get you started.

Outdoor Destinations

In the first section, we'll go together to places that are worth a chunk of your day, and that are worth traveling across town to visit if you're hungry for green spaces. Each is a place to sooth your soul... and to provide space for the younger members of your tribe to run off some of their excess energy.

The Bronx Zoo (International Wildlife Conservation Center)
This is one of the great zoos of the world. The zoo is home to more than 6,000 animals. Everyone will insist on visiting the remarkable Congo Gorilla Forest, one of the world's largest concentrations of lowland gorillas, with more than 300 gorillas in all. Everyone wants to be there when they feed the penguins (3:30 P.M. daily) or the sea lions (10:30 A.M. and 3 P.M.). Most kids will want to start at the south end of the zoo, where they can see African animals—giraffes, lions, gorillas, baboons, and so on. Work your way north for the snakes, bears, elephants, wild horses, and those hungry penguins and sea lions. The zoo is open 365 days a year, but if you're on a budget, visit on Wednesday, when everyone is admitted free. *[Bronx River Pkwy. and Fordham Rd., The Bronx. Subway 2, 5: Bronx Park Ave. (south end of the park) or Pelham Pkwy. (north end) Free on Wed.]*

You'll find other zoos in the city. They are much smaller, of course, than the internationally-acclaimed Bronx Zoo, but may be more accessible to small children and worth a stop if you're nearby:

The **Central Park** zoo is described in Chapter 16.

Prospect Park *[450 Flatbush Ave., Brooklyn. Subway F, Q, S: Prospect Park; 2, 3: Brooklyn Museum.]*. This is a small one, but there are sea lion feedings at 11:30, 2, and 4.

Corona Park *[53-51 111th St., Queens. Subway 7: 111th St.]*. This is also small, but the obligatory sea lion meals are at 11:15, 2:15, and 4:15.

Staten Island *[614 Broadway, Staten Island. From the Staten Island Ferry, take bus S48 and get off at Forest Avenue and Broadway.*

The zoo is a 5-minute walk south on Broad-way] has a fine children's center, a great snake exhi-bition, and a good variety of other animals.

Don't miss your golden opportunity to visit Brooklyn's Prospect Park

New York Botanical Garden
Here's a stop that might sound like a long shot for some families. Our kids would *not* have wanted to go to a botanical garden when they were small! So sometimes we went to a place like that and told them it was a park! Fair enough. That's what botanic gardens are—really cool parks! There's no more beautiful place for a day outdoors.

Only Kew, England, and Montreal, Canada, have larger and more spectacular gardens than this! The 250-acre park is filled with thousands of exotic plants that can't be seen anywhere else in one place: rain forest and tropical plants, arctic and tundra plants, desert plants, a veritable world tour. Kids will gasp at giant fronds that look like they're about to gobble someone up. Even if you have children who can't be bothered with flowers, it won't take them long to get into the spirit of the place, seeing bananas, smelling spices, and wandering around in a park that you just won't believe is in New York City. *[200th St. & Kazimiroff Blvd., The Bronx. Subway D: Bedford Park; 4: Allerton Ave. or take a train from Grand Central. The Metro-North Harlem Line stops in front of the main gate. Closed Mon.]*

You'll find other botanical gardens in New York, too, but the one to visit if you're nearby is the **Brooklyn Botanic Garden**

New York City for Families

[1000 Washington Ave., Brooklyn. Subway Q, S: Prospect Park; 2, 3, 4, 5: Franklin Ave.; S: Botanic Garden. Closed Mon.] This is a treat. We've seen kiwi fruit growing along the path in the winter, enjoyed the Japanese Garden and Cherry Esplanade, and Bonsai Museum, and taken pictures in the greenhouse of one cactus that looked exactly like Mickey Mouse! The BBG is only one-fifth as large as the huge gardens in the Bronx, but we like it because it's so easily accessible and is still more than large enough for a delightful afternoon.

Prospect Park

Manhattan's Central Park isn't the only big public park in New York. If you're in Brooklyn, a visit to Prospect Park is a must. We've already talked about Brooklyn Museum (Chapter 15), the zoo in the park, and the adjacent botanic garden, but there's much more to see and do in this park that's been the soul of Brooklyn for almost 150 years.

It would be nearly as easy to devote a chapter to Prospect Park as it was to Central Park. You can easily spend the day there and the activities are just as varied... and often just the same! Like Central Park, Prospect Park has a marvelous old **Carousel** (this one from 1912 and costing just 50 cents to ride). There's an ice skating rink in the winter (called, like the one in Manhattan, **Wollman Rink**). There's a large lake here for boating and fishing, a bandshell and the **Music Pagoda** that are among the nicest places in the city for enjoying the performing arts, countless playgrounds and ball fields, fabulous scenery—it's a terrific family place.

But the park has unique attractions of its own. The architecture of the **Boathouse** and the **Tennis House** is some of the most attractive and genteel in the city. (Curiously, there's no boating at the Boathouse, which is undergoing an extensive restoration, and no tennis at the Tennis House, which is headquarters of an environmental organization.)

New York's largest expanse of green, the aptly-named **Long Meadow**, runs a mile through the heart of the park. The park hosts a marketplace each Sunday from May to October... often accompanied by African drumming and dancing.

The **Lefferts Homestead Children's Historic House Museum** is a 200-year-old Dutch colonial farmhouse that features programs for kids as varied as sheep shearing, story telling, and weaving.

That doesn't do justice to it. Leave it at this. If you'd like a day in the park without all the fuss and fury of Manhattan, this is your choice. *[Prospect Park, Brooklyn. Subway 2, 3: Brooklyn Museum; F, Q, S: Prospect Park]*

Flushing Meadows-Corona Park
Yep, Prospect Park is your choice. Unless you'd prefer Queens and Flushing Meadows-Corona Park.

Sandwiched between the Asian communities of Flushing and the Hispanic neighborhoods of Corona, this huge double park has been the site of two world's fairs and is the home of an important art museum, a grand-slam tennis tournament, and much more.

One of the best meeting places in New York is in the very center of the park, the **Unisphere**, a 140-foot-tall (43m), 700,000-pound (318,000kg) stainless steel globe made for the 1964 World's Fair. It's by far the largest, but only one of several notable pieces of outdoor sculpture in the park.

Yes, you'll find a zoo, a carousel, the city's largest lake,

The dramatic Unisphere was built for the 1964 World's Fair

playgrounds galore, an ice rink, an outdoor theater. The park is home to the New York Hall of Science (Chapter 12), the Queens Museum of Art (Chapter 15), the National Tennis Center (which hosts the U.S. Open), Shea Stadium (home of the New York Mets baseball team), Queens Botanical Gardens, and many more things to see and do. *[Flushing Meadows-Corona Park, Queens. Subway 7: 111th St. or Willets Point-Shea Stadium]*

Brooklyn Heights Promenade
This is a bit different. Here is a soothing spot with no open green space and no recreational activities, but it's one of our very favorite outdoor spots. The Promenade is a half-mile (.3km) long walkway that runs from Orange Street to Remsen Street along the East River on the western edge of Brooklyn. The view is one worth traveling across the city for.

From the Promenade you have one of the city's very best pieces of eye candy. The Brooklyn Bridge on your right stretches majestically across the river to Lower Manhattan, where the

In a city of spectacular views, none can beat the one from the Brooklyn Heights Promenade

twin towers of the World Trade Center, the majestic Woolworth Building, and dozens of other skyscrapers soar. Look upriver to see the regal high-rises of Midtown.

There's no real park here, but there is a playground (with public toilets) near the south end of the walk. Better still, there's usually an ice cream truck parked there. It's a historic spot, too, site of George Washington's headquarters in August 1776 during the Battle of Long Island.

Best of all, though, are the benches. I can sit there reading, relaxing, and looking out over the river for as long as my companions will let me, enjoying the view and watching the people go by. You'll see lovers walking hand-in-hand or nuzzling on the benches,

> ***Tip:*** *Because you're looking west across the river, the view is at its finest in the morning, with the sun at your back, lighting the skyline, or after dark, when the countless lights of the city take over.*

kids tearing past at the speed only kids can travel, mothers pushing strollers, students studying, businessmen eating their lunches—I even watched a guy just taking his chainsaw for a walk late one morning, up and down the walkway. The Promenade is one of my *very* favorite places in a city where I have many favorites. [*Brooklyn Heights. Subway 2, 3: Clark St.; A, C: High St. Open until 1 A.M.*]

In the Swim of Things

Summer temperatures in New York City can be blisteringly hot. All that concrete reflects the sun, so you're getting it twice—once from above, once from below. One solution is to spend a lot of time in air-conditioned museums. But another is to go to the beach and let the ocean cool you off. The city has a number of places where you can get sand between your toes.

Brooklyn's **Coney Island** (Chapter 13) is a great day out and has a huge beach. Besides that, of course, there are about a million other ways to have fun at Coney, and on a hot day it can be more crowded than Times Square

If your plan is just to splash in the water and lie in the sun, and you don't want to battle the crowds, consider **Rockaway Park** *[Queens. Subway A to Broad Channel and change to S: Rockaway Park Beach]*. The trip can take an hour from Midtown on the A train, but the advantage is that you've got a 5-mile-long (8km) beach to frolic on and boardwalk to stroll. Crowds don't begin to approach the levels of the Brooklyn beaches. A bonus for the kids: a close-up view of the big planes in and out of JFK Airport, which is nearby.

Two other popular Brooklyn beaches are **Brighton Beach** *[Subway Q: Brighton Beach]* and **Manhattan Beach** *[use the same Subway station and walk a half-mile east along the esplanade, or hop on a B1 or B49 bus]*. These are also usually crowded in the summer because of their proximity to Coney Island.

Outdoor Diversions

The places above are all worth traveling across the city to visit. But there are others near wherever you are where you can spend a half hour or more with an interesting view, a bit of history, or a cool beverage. These are ideal places for kids to release energy hoarded by being good and speaking quietly in a museum, or for everybody to park under a tree and eat lunch. They exist in every neighborhood of every borough. Be on the lookout, too, for other quiet corners—churchyards, building courtyards and plazas, parks too small to be marked on your map. All can provide a welcome respite from all the effort it sometimes takes to have so much fun! Hundreds of places are available, but here I'll just point out some of my favorites in Manhattan, from south to north.

At the southern tip of Manhattan is **Battery Park** *[Battery. Subway 1, 9: South Ferry; 4, 5: Bowling Green; N, R: Whitehall St.]* where you can catch the ferries to the Statue of Liberty, Ellis Island, and Staten Island, see the old Castle Clinton fortress, and be within walking distance of many of the attractions in this book.

On the other hand, **Battery Park City** *[Along the Hudson River west of the World Trade Center, Lower Manhattan. Subway 1, 9, N, R: Rector St; 4, 5: Bowling Green]* isn't exactly a park at all, but a broad esplanade along the Hudson River, with a first-rate view of the harbor, the river, and the Statue of Liberty on one side and an equally inspiring view of Lower Manhattan on the other. It is one of the most memorable two-mile urban strolls in the world.

Battery Park is a fascinating example of old and new architecture side by side

Downtown is filled with parks ranging from the pleasant to the spectacular. **Two Bridges Park** *[Lower Manhattan near Chinatown. Subway 4, 5, 6: Brooklyn Bridge-City Hall]* sits between the Brooklyn and Manhattan bridges, offering a magnificent view of both. **Washington Square** *[W 4ᵗʰ St., Greenwich Village. Subway A, C, E, F, S: W. 4ᵗʰ St.-Washington Sq.]* is the hub and heart of Greenwich Village. Its arch is one of Lower Manhattan's best-loved landmarks. Don't play chess there unless you're serious about it. A few blocks away is

Tompkins Square [*E.7ᵗʰ St. and Ave. A, East Village. Subway 6: Astor Pl.*], a large peaceful park now that was often the scene of demonstrations and protests. **Union Square** [*E. 14ᵗʰ St. and Park Ave. South, Chelsea. Subway 4, 5, 6, L, N, R, Q, W: Union Sq.-14ᵗʰ St.*] hosts Manhattan's best farmers' market.

Pretty **Madison Square** [*E. 23ʳᵈ St. and Madison Ave., Chelsea. Subway N, R: 23ʳᵈ St.*] is as peaceful a place as you can find in Manhattan, with its lush trees (as contrasted with the lushes that a few other parks attract) and appealing view of the Flatiron Building. **Bryant Park** [*W. 42ⁿᵈ St. and Avenue of the Americas, Midtown. Subway B, D, F, S: 42ⁿᵈ St.*] sits behind the Public Library. It's a haven for lunch-munchers during the day and for film buffs on summer evenings, who gather for the free movies shown in the park.

The **Peace Garden** [*E. 47ᵗʰ St. and First Ave., Midtown. Subway 4, 5, 6, 7, S: Grand Central*] sits beside the United Nations buildings and has an inspiring view of these monuments to human aspirations... and the East River.

Riverside Park [*along the Hudson River from 69ᵗʰ St. to 125ᵗʰ St. Subway 1, 9: many stations*] seems to stretch forever along the West Side. It offers fine river views and a variety of attractions and notable buildings along the way. At the northern end of Manhattan is **Fort Tryon Park** [*W. 190ᵗʰ St., Subway A: 190ᵗʰ St.*]. We go up here for the Cloisters art museum, but like to stroll through the park, too, where there are the remnants of a Revolutionary War fort, some wonderful overlooks, and some unusual outdoor art.

I could go on for many more pages, but you'll have no trouble discovering *your* favorite outdoor spots. Visitors are always surprised that New York City has so much green space. Don't be surprised: You've been warned.

Recommendations

✔ New York has a lot of wonderful indoor activities, but there is *so* much else to life! Spend time outdoors, no matter what the weather or time of year.

✔ Visit parks along one of the rivers for memorable views

✔ Spend a minimum of one day at a park, garden, beach, or zoo for every week of your visit.

For the latest updates to *New York City for Families*, check out our page on the web at:

www.interlinkbooks.com/nycforfamilies.html

Chapter 18 Highlights

18. Shopping Streets

N ow I'll start out by saying that shopping for its own sake is something I don't entirely understand. Buying—yes. If you want or need something, you have to buy it, unless you've got a lot of friends who give you things. But shopping just to meander through stores looking at more or less the same merchandise... well, the excitement of that escapes me. I'll make exceptions, though, and even I will admit that shopping in New York City can be a lot of fun.

When we travel, you can count on our spending at least an afternoon strolling along the main shopping street of a city, or sampling its most famous shops a la carte. We're not really looking for souvenirs because as often as not we don't buy anything at all on these excursions. But shopping streets are a great place to people-watch, and they're an exceptional place to stimulate your imagination.

If anybody in your family likes to shop, better lock up the credit cards when you get to New York, because temptations abound. I don't want to make trouble, but in the next few pages I'm going to talk about places that are fun even for a non-shopper like me. And if they're fun for *me*, they will be heaven on earth for anybody who really likes to shop. One caveat as you start to walk: Stores do move, and if one of the neat places I've mentioned has shifted locations since my last visit, it's probably been replaced by something even cooler.

Midtown Shopping

This is where the fun starts—two of the greatest shopping streets in the world are right here... Fifth Avenue and Madison Avenue. If you're visiting in December, it's great fun just to walk down the street gawking at holiday window displays that cost more to erect than your annual salary. Fun if you don't think about that part, anyhow. But at any time of year, this is the best place in New York just to window shop.

I can't possibly provide a complete catalog of all the stores and boutiques on these streets, but I can give you a taste of a few of the places some of your family members might like to peek into. Or melt down their credit cards in.

Fifth Avenue

What a place to start! In fact, many shoppers never get beyond Fifth Avenue—it's the beginning and end of their excursion. It's not hard to see why there's little need to go further afield. Let's begin at Grand Army Plaza, the southeast corner of Central Park, cross 59th Street so we're walking on the left-hand side, and stroll south, away from the park. We can't possibly go into every elegant or intriguing store along the way—we don't have nearly enough time... or money. But I'll point out some of the places one or another family member might like to investigate.

A great place to start would be **FAO Schwarz**, one of the greatest toy stores anywhere. It's on our side of the street and if we've got kids along, this could be our one and only stop of the day. It's like Christmas morning here all year long. The company has been in business since 1862, so they must know something about what children like. Say hello to the giant teddy bear next to the door as you enter and start making your gift list now. The

*The kids will insist on stopping at the amazing toy store
FAO Schwartz*

store is a riot of color and sound with more activity going on than in a three-ring circus. And if you're unsure of anything, they've even got "Toy Demonstrators."

After you cross 58th Street you'll see **Bergdorf Goodman** on the other side of the street at No. 754, a very elegant store with a huge variety of designer clothes for women. The equally fashionable men's store is on our side of the street, next to a building that used to house the Warner Brothers Store, now moved to Times Square. But you can still see the cartoon characters on the side of the building.

Now we cross the street, and we're really getting to the good stuff... if you brought your life savings. **Tiffany & Co.** is right here at No. 727. If the glitter here isn't enough, next door is the **Trump Tower** and one of the elegant shops here is **Cartier**. Less expensive and (fortunately) more interesting to most kids is **Niketown**, on 57th Street just around the corner. You'll also find

There's great shopping at the big department stores

Tower Records in the lower garden level of the Trump Tower. In the next block there are several places you might not want to take kids into, but the **Disney Store** is down the block on our side of the street. There was a Coca Cola Store next door for a long time, but it's now just office for the company.

Now we'll cross 55th Street and consider stopping in **Christian Dior**, **Godiva Chocolates**, and **Elizabeth Arden** as we hurry by. (I can never make it past Godiva, I'm afraid.) Cross the next street and consider **Gucci** and several other temptations in the next couple of blocks. Sports fans will certainly want to check out the **NBA Store** at 52nd Street and Fifth Avenue. **Gianni Versace** is just across 52nd Street, but we can go a block further and stop in St. Patrick's Cathedral to pray for the strength to resist the enticements of the neighborhood.

Because we're not finished yet! We cross 50th Street and we have arrived at **Saks Fifth Avenue**. We, or at least our budgets, are indeed lost. Oh, there's more. In the next few blocks we'll find some very delectable jewelers across the street, though some kids might rather spend time at the big **HMV** record store past 47th (thank goodness!). There's much, much more, but you have the idea.

If you start at Central Park and make it this far down in just a single afternoon, my hat is off to you. And you'll probably have enough money to be able to get home at the end of your holiday.

> **Tip:** Some of the best shopping in the city is at the museums. Museum shops have unique, tasteful gifts and souvenirs and reproductions of objects in their collections, as well as posters, books, CDs, science toys, and things you won't find anywhere else. The shop at the Met is a destination in itself.

Madison Avenue

We could do the same thing on this street that we did with Fifth Avenue—just go block by block and point out a tiny smattering of the best places, but maybe we won't go into *quite* as much detail this time. You've got the idea.

Madison Avenue is a real haven for designer clothes and accessories. Families with more than one teenage girl are hereby warned to stay on the other side of town. If you head north from the Sony Building at 56th Street and Madison Avenue, you'll hit all the highlights.

I like to look at the **Mont Blanc** store at No. 593, where pens (They prefer to call them "writing instruments") can cost more money than I make as a teacher in a month. The kids would probably prefer to go across the street to **Eddie Bauer**. If you're in need of a watch, look for the branches of **Tourneau** along Madison Avenue—at 52nd, 57th, and 59th streets. The one at 57th is the largest watch store in the world.

There are lots of good places to browse across 60th Street—**DKNY** is popular with kids and **Calvin Klein** is hard to pass by, but also look at **Barney's**. No dinosaurs here, but an eclectic selection of interesting clothes and merchandise. At 66th Street there are tasty morsels to make you drool at the **Madison Gourmet Grocery**.

For western wear try **Billy Martin's** (started by the former Yankee manager) at 68th Street. Above 70th is **Yves St. Laurent** and the luscious **Cashmere-Cashmere**, and a couple of **Ralph Lauren** stores grace the next block.

Oh, you can go on forever, or for as long as your legs and credit line last, block after block, all the way to **Doll House Antics**, a wonderful dollhouse and miniature store at 96th Street.

Still More Stores

You don't have to be a hard-core shopper to want to visit **Macy's**, the largest store in the world. *[151 W. 34th St. at Broadway, Chelsea. Subway B, D, F, Q, N, R, S, W: 34th St. Open until 8:30 p.m. except 7 p.m. Sun.]* The 11-story building (or, rather, series of connected buildings) holds merchandise of every imaginable description and is a tourist attraction in itself—quite a change from the little dry-goods store that, on its first day of business in 1857, had total sales of just $11.06!

Of course the best time to visit Macy's is in November and December. The holiday season begins in America on Thanksgiving Day, in late November, with the enormous Macy's Thanksgiving Day Parade. The three-hour parade has been a tradition since 1924, and runs from 77th Street and Central Park West, to Columbus Circle, then down Broadway to Macy's, where it turns on 34th Street and ends at Seventh Avenue. Hundreds of thousands of people line the streets and tens of millions more watch on television.

The giant parade balloons are inflated the night before, when 77th and 81st streets are closed west of Central Park for the event. Visitors are welcome to watch between 6 and 11 P.M.

Macy's holiday windows are a tourist attraction in themselves. There is no better "window shopping" in the world and if the displays and animations don't entice you into the store, there's no hope for you as a shopper.

And of course you couldn't visit New York City in December without stopping in to sit on Santa's lap at Macy's (although Santa really hates it when *I* do that). Getting a billion or so kids through the line to give Santa their wish lists is an extraordinary feat of logistics, and if a single, albeit magical, elf really could take care of all those children, that would be the *real* "Miracle on 34th Street." But there's a secret that kids never find out: Santa brings helpers. I'll let a friend tell her story: *Yes, we actually stood in line for 2½ hours to see the Macy's Santa Claus. That was because our 6-year-old couldn't be deterred. Of course, the children didn't know it but there were actually 11 Santas listening to Christmas wishes. They had several "mazes" lined with Christmas stuff that led to "your" Santa. None of the kids was the wiser.*

Macy's is just across the street from the Empire State Building, so you'll probably get there without having to make a separate trip. But you won't really have been to New York unless you've shopped at Macy's.

> ***Tip:*** *Macy's is so vast that it can be hard to find what you want. So make your first stop the store's Visitor Center on the 34th Street balcony to pick up store maps and directories or talk to a store guide about where to find just what you're looking for.*

If you want to hit *all* the famous department stores, don't skip **Bloomingdale's** *[1000 Third Ave. at E. 59th St., Upper East Side. Subway 4, 5, 6: 59th St.; N, R: Lexington Ave. Open until 8:30 p.m. (7 p.m. Sat. and Sun.)]*. You can't buy hoop skirts—the store's original specialty—any more, but you can find almost anything else. Bloomingdale's cultivates an upper-crust image, and it doesn't hurt that it attracts the rich and famous, as well as people like you and me. Even Great Britain's Queen Elizabeth II has stopped there to shop. Maybe she was just after one of the store's famous designer shopping bags to show off on the plane on her flight home.

Malls and Complexes

No one can really *shop* New York City. If you want to compress the experience as much as possible, though, there are some great

The splendid glass atrium at the World Financial Center is an ideal place to take a break from shopping

clusters of places to browse. You'll find small boutiques, big department stores, international chain stores, restaurants, outlet stores—the gamut of possibilities. No sense in listing all the stores here: You'll see a lot of familiar names, and a lot of o n e - o f - a - k i n d places. Besides, if you're a dedicated shopper, the fun is in discovering what a new place has available. Just go and enjoy.

Lower Manhattan has two terrific indoor complexes. First is the **World Trade Center** *[Subway 1, 9, N, R: Cortland St.; E: World Trade Center]*. This is not only a complex of offices where tens of thousands of people work each day, it's a city in itself. You can wander around the lower level for days, going in and out of hundreds of stores selling everything imaginable. Just a short stroll across a walkway is the **World Financial Center** where the high-end stores only number in the dozens. But the setting is spectacular. The 120-foot-tall (37m) glass Winter Garden features soaring live Palm trees and a magnificent marble staircase. Its towering wall of glass looks out over a marina and the Hudson River, and its esplanade down to Battery Park City. If anybody else wants to shop, that's okay with me. I'll just buy a cup of gourmet coffee, sit on a bench, and admire the view.

Near the Empire State Building you're bound to see references to the **Manhattan Mall**. [*W. 33rd St. at Sixth Ave., Chelsea. Subway B, D, F, Q, N, R, S, W: 34th St.; 1, 2, 3, 9: Penn Station-34th St. Open until 8 p.m. except 6 p.m. Sun.*] This is a complex of more than 60 stores that has the same familiar names you'll find in malls everywhere, with a few local attractions added. That's okay, if you're looking for something familiar, but there's more adventure a couple of blocks away at Macy's.

Neighborhoods

You'll find shopping complexes everywhere; New York is *very* good at providing opportunities to separate people from their money—visitors and residents alike. It's great fun to pick a dry afternoon and just browse through a neighborhood. Shoppers can shop, sightseers can see sights, kids can try out playgrounds. It's a relaxed time.

Try **Soho**, especially along Broadway and intersecting streets between Houston and Broome streets [*Subway 1, 9: Houston St.; A, C, E: Canal St.*]. This is also prime territory for small galleries and stylish boutiques.

Greenwich Village is an amazing mix of places—from bookstores, cafés, boutiques and specialty shops, funky clothing stores, discount outlets, and music stores to a few spots with tattoo and body piercing studios and the sort of toy stores you do *not* want your kids to browse in. Take in the area around Washington Square, especially wandering in and out of the shops along 8th Street. [*Subway A, C, E, F, S: W. 4th St.-Washington Sq.; N, R: 8th St-NYU*]

Visitors never associate the Lower East Side with serious shopping, but that's where you'll find the **Bargain District**, billed as "New York's original outlet center." *[Subway F: Delancey St.; J, M, Z: Essex St.]* The streets around Orchard and Delancey streets have scores of shops with original, inexpensive, and interesting goods. It's a great neighborhood to eat in, too. The famous Katz's Deli is there, but you'll also find delicious international treats within a five-minute walk of wherever you happen to be standing. (Quick check of my notes: Chinese, Indian, Italian, French, Turkish, Japanese, vegetarian, Greek, Thai—and those are just the ones I noticed!)

Escape from Manhattan and browse Brooklyn's **Fulton Mall** *[Subway 2, 3: Hoyt St.; M, N, Q, R: DeKalb Ave.]*, a long pedestrian thoroughfare with shops ranging from Macy's to places selling the hippest, funkiest clothes and music. At the east end of the Mall you can visit a Brooklyn institution— *Junior's Restaurant [386 Flatbush Ave.]*. Understand that I'm getting into controversial territory here, but it might not be going too far to say that the best cheesecake in the world is made right here. New York is *the* place for cheesecake, and while every New Yorker has his or her own favorite, Junior's is probably the most acclaimed.

Perhaps this is a good place to end this chapter, sitting at a window table in Junior's, finishing off a late post-shopping lunch of a mammoth hamburger and homemade sweet potato french fries with a six-inch-tall slab of chocolate mousse cheesecake. And now that this image is in my mind, I find I have nothing left to say, so will concentrate on my lunch.

You won't lack for shopping opportunities in New York City. Your only problem will be making time for the *other* things you want to do.

Recommendations

✔ Window shop your way through a neighborhood. It's fun and free.

✔ Visit one of the big department stores, especially if you're in New York in December.

✔ Make a point of at least ogling some of the very expensive, exclusive shops. The prices will give you conversation material for weeks.

For the latest updates to *New York City for Families*,
check out our page on the web at:

www.interlinkbooks.com/nycforfamilies.html

Part III
Planning Pages

The idea of *New York City for Families* is to make your holiday as easy and hassle-free as possible. This section is where it all comes together. By now everyone has read and talked about how to Live Like a Local in Part I and considered all the excitement New York offers in Part II. Everybody's convinced this will be the trip of a lifetime. Now it's time to polish the plans. Chapter 19 presents a comprehensive list of the attractions in this book, perfect for marking, voting, or just discussing. Chapter 20 lays out one- and two-week itineraries—not to set your agenda for you, but to show you some ways to plan and pace a trip like this. Chapter 21 helps you figure your budget—travel, accommodations, and your total spending—so you can get the most for your money. And the appendix lists more than 120 sites on the Web where you can get more information, make travel and accommodations arrangements, and fine-tune your trip.

Now we've got the total package: What to do, how to do it, and budgeting for it. All that's left is for you to pack your suitcases and get on with a trip your whole family will remember and talk about for years to come. May your travels be as fun and as memorable as ours have been.

19. Attractions

We could keep piling on museums and parks and exhibits almost forever. I've had to leave so much out! Interesting museums, historic buildings, cool video arcades. Some good places are just too remote and time-consuming for a short-term visitor. Others duplicate too much of what is already here, or perhaps have too narrow an appeal. But we've covered more than 180 attractions in the earlier chapters, and that ought to be enough to give any family a good start. If you finish all these during your first week in the city, you'll have to spend all of the second one recovering anyway!

Seriously, there's enough here to keep you busy for several trips. So how can you possibly choose what to do in the limited time you have available?

This is a *family* trip; everybody needs a voice. If Mom and Dad make all the decisions, you're courting disaster.

I suggested earlier that every family member who is old enough to read chapters 10-18 do so. That will give everybody at least 180 ideas for things they can't wait to do—and things they definitely do *not* want to do! You need to talk together about what's most important, what would be most fun, and what would be nice... but could be left out, if necessary.

Attractions

The Lains were probably over-organized about the planning but here's a technique that worked for us. Maybe you don't need to do it in the same way, but however you approach the planning, keep the principles from Chapter 9 in mind: Everybody gets his or her first choice, everybody is tolerant of everyone else's first choice, and this is a *family* trip.

After reading and talking about our destination for several weeks, we prepared as comprehensive a list as we could of all the possible attractions and activities. We made a copy of the list for each family member, both parents and kids, and asked everybody to mark each item on the list in one of three ways:

- I really want to see/do this
- I don't care about this one way or the other
- I don't find this interesting at all

We also asked each person to mark the *one* attraction or activity he or she thought was most important, the thing that it would be really disappointing to miss.

Then we tallied up the votes. Some things everybody liked and those went to the top of our itinerary. Things no one wanted to do were struck off. But we stuck to our rule: If anybody listed an item as his or her most important attraction, it went to the top of the list, even if nobody else voted for it at all.

Once we had a list of what we *wanted* to do, we had to work out what was *possible*, and plan a rough itinerary. The next chapter will help with that. But we *always* left time to relax and take some time off, and we *always* left plenty of opportunities to change our minds in case some unexpected possibility presented itself, as it almost always did. (For example, once in Montreal, I had a chance encounter with a baseball player who had been a childhood hero of mine, now a broadcaster for my favorite team, which was in town at the time. We struck up a conversation and when we parted, he asked if we'd like to go to the game the next night. He left box seat tickets for us at the stadium and we were delighted to change our plans and see the game.)

Whatever system you use, if everybody is involved in the planning, everybody will have a personal stake in the success and smooth operation of the trip.

On the next few pages is a list of all the attractions we've talked about in the earlier chapters. You can make copies of these pages for each member of the family to vote on, or just use them as an outline for the family discussions. The chapters in which each was featured is in brackets, if you'd like to refresh your memories, and I've highlighted in **bold** type the attractions that probably have the widest appeal to most families.

One more thing: I've marked the items outside Manhattan with the borough each is located in. I've said it before: Get out of Manhattan sometimes. Almost one-fourth of all the attractions in this book are outside Manhattan, and you won't *really* have been to New York unless you see something of the rest of the city.

Get out of Manhattan and into the other boroughs

Attractions

- ❏ American Museum of the Moving Image [14] *(Queens)*
- ❏ **American Museum of Natural History [12]**
- ❏ Americas Society [11]
- ❏ Apollo Theater [11, 14]
- ❏ Asia Society [11]
- ❏ Bargain District [18]
- ❏ Battery Park [17]
- ❏ Battery Park City [17]
- ❏ Bloomingdale's [18]
- ❏ Brighton Beach [17] *(Brooklyn)*
- ❏ **Bronx Zoo (International Wildlife Conservation Center) [17] *(The Bronx)***
- ❏ Brooklyn Academy of Music [14] *(Brooklyn)*
- ❏ Brooklyn Botanic Garden [17] *(Brooklyn)*
- ❏ **Brooklyn Bridge [10] *(Brooklyn-Manhattan)***
- ❏ Brooklyn Children's Museum [12] *(Brooklyn)*
- ❏ **Brooklyn Heights Promenade [17] *(Brooklyn)***
- ❏ Brooklyn Museum of Art [15] *(Brooklyn)*
- ❏ Bryant Park [17]
- ❏ **Bus Ride [6, 13]**
- ❏ Carnegie Hall [6, 14]
- ❏ Cathedral of St. John the Divine [10]
- ❏ **Central Park [6, 16]**
  - ❏ Belvedere Castle
  - ❏ Bethesda Fountain
  - ❏ Blockhouse No. 1
  - ❏ Carousel
  - ❏ Central Park Wildlife Center (Zoo)
  - ❏ Charles A. Dana Discovery Center
  - ❏ Chess and Checkers House
  - ❏ Conservatory Garden
  - ❏ Conservatory Water
  - ❏ Dairy, The

❑ Delacorte Musical Clock
❑ Delacorte Theatre
❑ Harlem Meer
❑ Lake, The
❑ Lasker Rink and Pool
❑ Mall, The
❑ Obelisk
❑ Pond, The
❑ Ramble, The
❑ Reservoir, The
❑ Shakespeare in Central Park
❑ Swedish Cottage Marionette Theatre
❑ Tisch Children's Zoo
❑ Wollman Rink
❑ Chelsea Piers [13]
❑ Children's Museum of Manhattan [12]
❑ Chinatown [11]
❑ Chinatown Ice Cream Factory [11]
❑ Chrysler Building [10]
❑ Cloisters, The [15]
❑ Coney Island [13, 17] *(Brooklyn)*
❑ Astroland
❑ Deno's Amusement Park
❑ Nathan's Famous Hot Dogs
❑ Sideshows by the Seashore
❑ Ed Sullivan Theater [14]
❑ **Ellis Island [11]**
❑ **Empire State Building [6, 10]**
❑ FAO Schwarz [18]
❑ Federal Hall [15]
❑ Fifth Avenue [6, 18]
❑ Flatiron Building [10]

Attractions

- Flushing Meadow/Corona Park [17] *(Queens)*
  - Corona Park Zoo
  - Queens Botanical Gardens
  - Queens Museum of Art
  - Unisphere
- Forbes Magazine Galleries [15]
- Fort Tryon Park [17]
- Fraunces Tavern [15]
- Frick Collection [15]
- Fulton Mall [18] *(Brooklyn)*
- **Grand Central Terminal [6, 10]**
- Greenwich Village [18]
- Guggenheim Museum [10, 15]
- Guggenheim Museum Soho [15]
- Hard Rock Café [6]
- Harlem [11]
- Historic Richmond Town [15] *(Staten Island)*
- *Intrepid* Sea Air Space Museum [12]
- Japan Society Gallery [11]
- Jewish Museum [11]
- Junior's Restaurant [18] *(Brooklyn)*
- **Lain Walking Tour of Midtown [6]**
- Lazer Park [13]
- Lincoln Center [14]
- Little Italy [11]
- Lower East Side Tenement Museum [11]
- **Macy's [6, 18]**
- Madison Avenue [18]
- Madison Square [17]
- Madison Square Garden [13, 14]
- Manhattan Beach [17] *(Brooklyn)*
- Manhattan Mall [18]
- Marriott Marquis [6, 10]

❑ **Metropolitan Museum of Art** [15]
❑ MTV Studios [14]
❑ Museo del Barrio [11]
❑ Museum for African Art [11]
❑ Museum of American Folk Art [11]
❑ Museum of Chinese in the Americas [11]
❑ Museum of the City of New York [15]
❑ Museum of Jewish Heritage [11]
❑ Museum Mile [12]
❑ Museum of Modern Art [15]
❑ Museum of Television and Radio [14]
❑ Nathan's Famous Hot Dogs [13] *(Brooklyn and elsewhere)*
❑ National Museum of the American Indian [11]
❑ National Tennis Center [13] *(Queens)*
❑ NBA Store [18]
❑ New York Aquarium [13] *(Brooklyn)*
❑ New York Botanical Garden [17] *(The Bronx)*
❑ New York City Police Museum [12]
❑ NYC Fire Museum [12]
❑ **New York Hall of Science** [12] *(Queens)*
❑ New York Historical Society [15]
❑ New York Public Library [6, 15]
❑ New York Skyride [13]
❑ New York Transit Museum [12] *(Brooklyn)*
❑ Niketown [18]
❑ Off and Off-off Broadway [14]
❑ Old Merchant's House [15]
❑ P.S.1 [15] *(Queens)*
❑ Peace Garden [17]
❑ **Picnic in the Park** [5]
❑ Plaza Hotel [10]
❑ Pro Sports [13]
   ❑ N.Y. Knicks

Attractions

- ❏ N.Y. Liberty
- ❏ N.Y. Mets *(Queens)*
- ❏ N.Y. Rangers
- ❏ N.Y. Yankees *(The Bronx)*
- ❏ Brooklyn Cyclones *(Brooklyn)*
- ❏ Prospect Park [17] *(Brooklyn)*
  - ❏ Boathouse
  - ❏ Carousel
  - ❏ Lefferts Homestead Museum
  - ❏ Tennis House
  - ❏ Wollman Rink
- ❏ Radio City Music Hall [14]
- ❏ Riverside Church [10]
- ❏ Riverside Park [17]
- ❏ Rockaway Park [17] *(Queens)*
- ❏ Rockefeller Center [6, 10, 14]
- ❏ Rockefeller Plaza skating [6, 13]
- ❏ **Roosevelt Island Tram [13]**
- ❏ St. Patrick's Cathedral [6, 10]
- ❏ St. Paul's Chapel [15]
- ❏ Saks Fifth Avenue [6, 18]
- ❏ Shea Stadium [13] *(Queens)*
- ❏ Snug Harbor Cultural Center [13] *(Staten Island)*
- ❏ Soho [18]
- ❏ Sony Wonder Technology Lab [13]
- ❏ **South Street Seaport [15]**
- ❏ Staten Island Ferry [6, 13] *(Staten Island-Manhattan)*
- ❏ Staten Island Institute of Arts and Sciences [13] *(Staten Island)*
- ❏ Staten Island Zoo [17] *(Staten Island)*
- ❏ **Statue of Liberty [10]**
- ❏ Studio Museum in Harlem [11]
- ❏ Temple Emanu-el [10]
- ❏ Theater District [6]

❏ Tiffany & Co [18]
❏ **Times Square [6, 10, 14]**
❏ TKTS Booths [6, 14]
❏ Tompkins Square [17]
❏ Trinity Church [15]
❏ Two Bridges Park [17]
❏ Union Square [17]
❏ United Nations [10, 11]
❏ Waldorf Astoria [10]
❏ Washington Square [17]
❏ Whitney Museum of American Art [15]
❏ World Financial Center [18]
❏ World Trade Center [10, 18]
❏ Yankee Stadium [13] *(The Bronx)*

20. Sample Itineraries

The only people who can see *everything* on a trip to New York are biologists who have managed to clone hundreds of copies of themselves. If you're not a family of Nobel-Prize-winning biologists, though, you'll just have to accept the idea that you can't see and do it all. In fact, if you want this to be a relaxing family vacation rather than an ordeal that causes more stress than it relieves, you should probably try to do *less* than you expect.

You'll enjoy it more.

Pacing is critical on a family trip to a new place. You want to get your money's worth and see all the famous highlights, plus the special things that really appeal to you, but if you set too relentless a tempo, people will feel like they're spending all their time on the subway, being herded from one place to the next. Everyone will start to get tired and grouchy, and you'll have to wait for the photos to come back so you can figure out where you went.

Most of the time, one activity before lunch, one after lunch (or two nearby ones) and one after dinner sometimes, is the most you ought to do.

What those activities are will depend on what your family likes, of course.

If your kids are really into zoos, New York City is a gold mine: There's a zoo in every borough. Manhattan, Brooklyn, and Staten Island have children's museums for the younger set. Science? The Hall of Science in Queens, the Natural History Museum on the Upper West Side, and the Sony Technology Labs in Midtown are just the beginning. Art? Don't even get me started on the possibilities!

As a practical matter, you'll probably vary your activities, and that's the best way to go. The checklist in the previous chapter will help establish some priorities.

The role of this chapter isn't to tell you how to spend your time, but to give you some ideas and, most importantly, show you a bit about how you can pace a trip if you haven't taken your family somewhere like this before. Spending a week in The Big City, with its myriad of attractions spread out over a couple of hundred square miles isn't much like taking a week's holiday to Disneyworld or the beach. The possibilities and permutations are almost infinite.

> ***Tip:*** *Remember the critical importance of making sure everyone gets their first choice. Plan those activities early in the trip in case weather, illness, or some other emergency causes a change of plans later. You don't want anybody to feel sad or disappointed that you didn't get to the one thing that really mattered to him or her.*

Of course the ages of the kids will be a factor. Little ones tire faster and need earlier bedtimes. Older teens might go off on their own sometimes. So take the itineraries below as starting points; add, subtract, and change things around so they suit your family's needs. It's *your* trip, after all. Just be sure to make the plans together, so it's *everybody's* trip.

The suggestions don't specify a day of the week, unless an attraction's opening hours require it. But remember that most attractions are closed one or two days a week. Always check to avoid disappointment. Mondays are usually lousy days to plan museum visits.

One-Week Itinerary

Arrival Day—First priority is to get organized, of course. You'll need to get moved into your accommodations and get unpacked. If you have an apartment or kitchenette you'll buy food. Get your subway passes at the nearest station. Best to get the necessary things out of the way immediately. Chapter 4 takes you step-by-step through the process. If you're an early morning arrival after an overnight flight, a short nap is essential, and might be for young kids no matter where they've come from. But eventually you'll be moved in and ready to see the sights. So which sights do you start with?

It's up to your family, of course. That's a great subject to discuss as you travel to help heighten the anticipation. But if I were asked to choose for most families, here's what I'd recommend.

Dive into the maelstrom of New York City with both feet. You're here—no point in just tiptoeing in. Take the Lain Walk in Chapter 6 and you'll see what you've come for... all the glitz and glamour of the city. The Lain Walk will take you past Central Park, through the heart of Times Square, past Macy's, in front of the Empire State Building, up fabulous Fifth Avenue, and back to where you started in just a couple of hours.

Of course the walk can last much longer than that. You're bound to be tempted to change directions when you see something neat, or to linger in Times Square, gawking at the signs, the people, or the buildings. That's okay! This isn't an endurance contest to see if you can finish the walk in the prescribed time. Maybe you'll get so distracted by something you'll *never* finish the walk. Fine. It happens to me all the time. I've been in New York City often and I *always* get distracted by new or exciting things when I walk through the area. I *always* linger in Times Square and everybody in *your* group will absolutely insist on it! That's why you're here. Remember: You don't have a time clock to punch—you're supposed to be having fun. I won't be offended if you *never* finish the walk.

Just one caveat: If you've been in the air for many hours, take it a bit easy on the walking until tomorrow; blisters hurt. Maybe you'll want to limit your first foray into the city to just Times Square, which probably is also the destination of choice for people who arrive too late in the day to take the full walk.

By now it's late afternoon or early evening and you're hungry. You can start cooking for yourself tomorrow. Tonight you've earned a good dinner. If you're still in the Times Square area, there are about a million places to eat nearby. They come in all price ranges and cuisines. Pick out two or three places *before* the rumbling of stomachs becomes the grumbling of companions.

After dinner you've got time, perhaps, for another stop before you head back. How about the Empire State Building? The wait will be shorter now than it was this afternoon, and the view at night is unforgettable. By the time you get there, wait your turn, and get to the top, the city should be lighting up. What a perfect end to your first day in New York!

But don't stay up too late tonight. You've been traveling and you have a busy week in store. No sense in getting run down at the beginning. Besides, you'll want an early start tomorrow.

A view of New York Harbor from Roosevelt Island

Sample Itineraries

Day 2—Isn't it splendid to wake up in this great city and know you've got days of fun ahead! All the preparation has been worth it. Don't sleep too late this morning: We've got something special planned. Grab breakfast and head for the subway. Unless the weather is really foul, we're going to the Statue of Liberty and an early start will beat the crowds.

If you can be at Battery Park by 8:30 or so, you can be on the first ferry out to Liberty Island and won't have to wait in lines. This is *really* worth getting up early for in the summer, when thousands of people come out here, but it's the best idea on *any* day of the year. The ferry takes about 15 minutes and the view of Lower Manhattan is spectacular. There's room to sit outside if the weather is nice, room inside if it's not. There are snacks, beverages, and toilets on board and the ride is smooth.

Enjoy the wonderful views of the statue and the city from the island, take the elevator to the museum or climb up to the crown if you're fit (or would like to be). It's a perfect way to begin the trip. Then, as long as you're out here, stop at Ellis Island for an hour on the way back. It's a wonderful, evocative place that will amaze most of your family with what millions of immigrants had to endure to move their own families to the United States.

By the time you get back to Battery Park it should be lunchtime. Maybe this would be a good day for lunch from a pushcart. Then move on to afternoon activities. If people enjoyed being out on the water, the Staten Island Ferry is nearby. My choice might be, though, to visit one of the neat attractions or neighborhoods in Lower Manhattan. The Tenement Museum would be a good follow-up to Ellis Island. Chinatown is fun and so is South Street Seaport. The American Indian Museum is a ten-minute walk away. Federal Hall and related historical sites from Chapter 15 are close. Or, if you didn't make it to the Empire State Building last night, the World Trade Center is just a five-minute subway ride from here.

Pick one or two things from this list.

You got up early this morning and have had an active day, so tonight just fix spaghetti at your apartment or hotel kitchenette and spend the evening relaxing at home.

Day 3—Yesterday was busy. Today you can slow the pace a little. Sleep late, have a good breakfast, and head to Central Park and environs for the day. You can spend as much time as you like in the park: Chapter 16 is filled with ideas. My favorite spots are probably the zoo, the Ramble, and the view from Belvedere Castle, but you might prefer the carousel, fishing in Harlem Meer, or a paddle boat on the lake. There's something for everybody. And this works summer or winter, although fishing and paddle-boating aren't good February activities, quite honestly.

Consider a late lunch. Take a picnic along or buy something from a snack bar, pushcart, or nearby pizza place (the pizza might be a better wintertime choice), and then take in a museum close to the park. The best choices might be the American Museum of Natural History, the Metropolitan Museum of Art, or the Manhattan Children's Museum, depending on what your kids are into.

This would be a great night to go to the theater, so stop by the TKTS booth after the museum. If you're not theater-goers, come back to Times Square tonight anyway, just for the lights.

Day 4—There is so much to see just in Midtown, you're starting to worry about how to fit it all in. There's nothing to worry about: You can't! But this might be a good day to split up for awhile. Do something together in the morning, and after lunch (if you haven't had New York-style pizza yet, *today's the day*) Mom and Dad can each take a kid or two and pursue separate interests, or the older kids might want to set off on their own for the afternoon.

What should we choose from in Midtown? Oh, my! The aircraft carrier *Intrepid* is a good choice, the Sony Wonder Technology Labs are fascinating, the Museum of Modern Art terrific, a backstage tour of Madison Square Garden or Radio City Music Hall great fun. This is a great time for people who like to shop to set off for Macy's or graze their way up Fifth Avenue. If you're on the East Side, check out Grand Central Terminal. Tour the United Nations. Ride the tram to Roosevelt Island and back. You have time for *only* one or two of these things. But whatever you do, you'll have plenty to share when you get back together at the apartment for dinner tonight.

If you want to go out again tonight, you might check for an inexpensive family off-off Broadway show. Or, if you haven't had a nighttime view of the city from a high perch, this could be a good night to go to the Empire State Building or World Trade Center if the weather is clear. If it's a summer evening, they might be showing a movie in Bryant Park behind the library. Or maybe you got tickets to a baseball, basketball, or hockey game. If you're going to Live Like a Local, remember that New Yorkers take their teams seriously!

Day 5—If you're on an international flight day after tomorrow, remember to call to reconfirm today.

I've been badgering you about getting out of Manhattan, into the boroughs. If you haven't done it yet, promise me you'll go today. Most tourists don't do it and they really miss out. But you're not a tourist—you're a temporary New Yorker!

A Day in Brooklyn: My choice would be to start the day at the City Hall subway station in Manhattan and walk across the Brooklyn Bridge. It's okay if you don't want to do that, but everybody will enjoy it if it's a nice morning. When the walkway ends at Tillary Street, walk a couple of blocks south to Borough Hall. There you can spend the morning shopping Fulton Mall (with lunch and cheesecake at Junior's) or visiting the Transit

Museum to learn about subways and buses. Then get on the subway for your next stop.

Take the 2 or 3 train to Grand Army Plaza for the war memorial arch and Prospect Park or one more stop to the Brooklyn Museum station for the Brooklyn Museum of Art, the Botanic Garden, or Prospect Park. If you want to go to the Brooklyn Children's Museum, the 3 train goes three more stops to Kingston Avenue, just a short walk from the museum. Any one or two of these will easily fill your afternoon.

Finish your day by taking the 2 or 3 train to Brooklyn Heights (or any bus to downtown Brooklyn) and spending a little time relaxing and gazing from the Brooklyn Heights Promenade. Watching Manhattan light up from this vantage point is a magical experience.

A Day in Queens: Our first destination of the day has got to be the terrific New York Hall of Science. The 7 train takes us to 111th Street, just a ten-minute stroll to the museum. (There's a little drugstore about halfway down the street where I stop to buy Band-Aids for my blisters.) An outing at the Hall of Science will take as much time as you care to give it, and if there are little ones in your troupe and you're visiting in the summer, you mustn't miss the best playground in New York, adjacent to the museum. Next you'll want to wander in Flushing Meadows-Corona Park, the site of two world's fairs. The Unisphere is worth a stop, and as long as you're there, pop into the Queens Museum of Art and see the enormous model of the city. There's nothing like it anywhere.

You might want to stay in the park for awhile; there's a zoo and botanic garden there, but when you leave, go by way of the National Tennis Center and Shea Stadium, just to see these temples of sport. Then get back on the 7 train and change to the G or R train at 74th St.-Broadway. Four stops will take you to Steinway Street and a five-minute walk gets you to the American Museum of the Moving Image. This is a nice afternoon of learning about motion pictures (and maybe seeing one of the screenings) and television in the same building where stars from Charlie Chaplin to Bill Cosby have worked. You'll have no trouble finding good places to eat in the area. Long Island City (where you are now) has a wide ethnic mix and restaurants to match. And if you want to try Greek food, nearby Astoria has the largest Greek population outside of Athens itself.

Day 6—This is such a depressing day: Our last full day in New York! There's still *so* much to do! Guess we'll just have to come back.

But how to spend the day? Well, you've probably got gaps to fill. Day 2 and Day 4 included much more than you could possibly do; go back and choose from those lists. Another good option might be to hit Museum Mile for part of the day, visiting two museums that look interesting. The Museum of the City of New York is a good choice: You know enough about the city to appreciate it now. Follow it up with something outdoors—part of Central Park you didn't get to a few days ago or, if it's not late, a ride out to the Bronx Zoo, one of the world's greatest wildlife centers.

Another good idea might be to go back downtown. You can stop in at the Fire and Police museums there and finding something good to have for lunch nearby will be no problem. And you can do all the last-minute shopping and souvenir-hunting you need all over Lower Manhattan. Finish the day by riding the ferry to Staten Island and back. It's free and you'll get one more terrific view of Manhattan to take with you when you leave. Then it's back to the apartment or hotel to pack. If you're flying, remember to put *all* your film—exposed and unexposed—back in your lead bag.

Departure Day—Not much time for sightseeing today. If you've got a plane to catch, you've got to leave well ahead of your departure time. If you drove, you've got a small window of reduced insanity between the morning and evening rush hours that it's in your interest to hit. Do stop somewhere and pick up a couple of bagels or a last pastrami sandwich to take along. It won't be a lasting memento of the trip, but it will help prolong the taste of New York just a little longer.

Two-Week Itinerary

If you're lucky enough to be staying for two weeks, you won't have to make as many compromises. You still can't see it all, but you won't have quite so many hard decisions to make.

> ___
> *Tip:* *Have backup plans. If the day you'd planned to spend at Coney Island is filled with pelting rain and lightning, visit some indoor destinations you'd planned for later in the trip and go to the beach tomorrow. Too foggy to see anything from the Empire State Building? Ride the Roosevelt Island tram or stroll along the Brooklyn Heights Promenade for impressive views.*

Day 1—I can't improve in the advice in the one-week itinerary above.

Day 2—Start out the same way, with the Statue of Liberty and Ellis Island. After lunch, follow the idea through by going to the South Street Seaport (an M15 bus from in front of the Staten Island Ferry terminal to Fulton Street is the easiest way) and talking about how amazing it was that early American settlers spent weeks crossing the ocean in ships like the ones moored there. (Remember, though, that most Ellis Island immigrants arrived later, on steamships.) If there's time, finish at the Tenement Museum (on the M15 bus again to Delancey Street).

Day 3—I still vote for Central Park today. It's worth spending all day, but if you want another activity this afternoon, see some art at the Met or up a bit further at the Guggenheim. The theater is still a good idea tonight.

Day 4—Midtown is still on the agenda today, focusing on the West Side and/or the theater district. People who want to shop should go to Macy's or up Fifth Avenue today. Actually, Fifth Avenue is fun for everybody if you didn't get here the first day. If you don't want to shop, watch the skaters at Rockefeller Plaza (late autumn to early spring), admire ornate St. Patrick's Cathedral, or just crane your neck to gawk at the buildings. Or try the *Intrepid*, Sony Labs, backstage tours or any of the other things listed above. Splitting into smaller groups might be a good idea today but a night out together as in the one-week itinerary would still be fun.

Day 5—You should really get out of Manhattan for at least one full day every week if you really want to say you've "done" New York City. Today, follow the Brooklyn option described above. Be sure to spend some time in Prospect Park or the botanic gardens. Tonight's evening event is to watch lower Manhattan light up from the Promenade.

Day 6—The last two days have been very big-city oriented. There's no place more big city than Midtown, and you won't mistake Brooklyn for an Iowa cornfield, either. So today is a day to commune with nature. From Grand Central it takes only about a half-hour to get to the Bronx Zoo, and it's hard to beat a day at the zoo—especially this one. When you're tired of the animals (I wouldn't know what that's like, myself. I love zoos.), the New York Botanical Gardens are nearby. You'll refuse to believe that you're in a city of 8 million people. A dose of fresh air, trees, and expansive grass will get you set up just right for your second week. If you're more into art than animals and the kids are interested in things medieval, you might go out to The Cloisters instead—for a half day, anyway. I can't think of a more beautiful place in New York. Spend the other half day working your way down the Upper West Side as far as the Natural History Museum. It might be a good idea to do a bit of laundry tonight to get you safely through the next week.

Day 7—Today let's plunge back into the urban environment. There's so much to see and do in Lower Manhattan, and many tourists don't see any of it. If I were planning for myself, I'd start out on Wall Street at Federal Hall, then visit as many of the historic sites in Chapter 15 as I had the legs for. You might prefer to see the Police and Fire museums, the American Indian Museum, or do some more shopping in Greenwich Village or the bargain district. Even if you're cooking dinner in your apartment most nights, go out to a nice restaurant tonight to celebrate the halfway point of your stay.

Day 8—This is a day that might be so fascinating to the kids that they won't notice how much they're learning. Call it Diversity Day. Start in Harlem (A or D to 125th St.) and stroll east down 125th Street. See what acts are coming to the Apollo Theater, check out the art at the Studio Museum of Harlem, turn up Lenox Avenue and study the menu at Sylvia's and decide if it's too early for lunch. Buy something colorful and fun to wear. Find some CDs you can't get at home. Your walk will be about a mile. If you get tired or are conserving your strength, any crosstown bus (M60, M100, M101, Bx15) can drop you off at Fifth Avenue. Catch an M1 bus and ride down to 104th to El Museo del Barrio and learn about the city's Latin heritage and culture.

Take the M1 further down Fifth Avenue to 68th and walk over to Park Avenue and you can find the Asia Society and the Americas Society within a block, if you like. But at either 104th or 68th, you'll want to return to the subway. Hop the 6 train downtown to Canal Street and spend the rest of the day in Chinatown. There are more places than this, of course. Substitute anything else from Chapter 11 into your day (or add it, if you're really relentless) and you have a day that would be difficult to duplicate anywhere else in the country.

Day 9—It's been five days since we focused on midtown, so maybe it's time to do the East Side. A tour if the United Nations would be a good follow-up to yesterday if the kids are old enough. You don't want to miss Grand Central, and a ride on the Roosevelt Island tram will provide great views. Inveterate shoppers will insist on a stop at Bloomingdale's and might spend some time on Madison Avenue. So this might be another opportunity to divide your forces. Somebody ought to go back to Times Square and visit the TKTS booth to see if you can get good tickets for a show tonight.

Day 10—Okay, time to get out of Manhattan again. This time follow the Queens suggestions from Day 5 one-week itinerary.

Day 11—Have you seen everything you're interested in along Museum Mile? If not, this is your chance. If so, maybe you'd like to take in Greenwich Village, if you didn't do that on Day 7. There's *so* much to see in Lower Manhattan. If it's a clear day and you're downtown anyway, a trip to the open-air roof of the World Trade Center might be in order. Finish your day with a trip on the Staten Island Ferry at sunset. The late afternoon sun will give the skyline a wonderful red glow. On your way back, the lights will be artificial... and every bit as worth seeing.

Day 12—If you're flying internationally, remember to confirm at least two days before departure.

If this is a summertime trip, you've got to go to the beach! If all you want to do is lie on the sand, race up and down the shore, and splash in the waves, Rockaway Park is ideal. It's relatively uncrowded, and as a bonus, you get a close-up view of the planes flying in and out of JFK. But for the full treatment, go to Coney Island. The "full treatment" of today is nothing compared to what it was 80 years ago, but it's still a great day out. Start the day at the Aquarium, look in on one of the odd sideshows along Surf Avenue, and stake out your spot on the beach by early afternoon. Make sure you're close enough to the arcades and rides and food stalls to ensure that you spend plenty of money! It really is a fun outing, and you'll want to stay until dark to watch the amusement parks light up.

Not a summer trip? The Aquarium is still worth a visit. Times Square has video arcades galore. If you're in a hotel, you might have a pool available, so you can have your own private beach party. Consider working off a little energy at Chelsea Piers, or go back to Brooklyn or Queens to pick up something you missed.

Day 13—Woe! It's almost over! We haven't even *begun* to see it all! If you didn't get to the American Museum of Natural History on Day 6, you need to go today. A trip to New York is hardly complete without a dinosaur or two. There are still art museums to visit, shopping streets to try, Times Square to hang out in one last time. Now is the time to check off anything on your must-do list that is still undone. Tonight you'll have to pack. But you'll have a lot of stories to tell when you get home.

Departure Day—Pretty much as outlined at the end of the one-week activity except you've had more time to shop. I hope someone remembered to bring an extra suitcase!

If you can stay more than two weeks, you certainly don't need any more advice from me. Every day I spend in New York City I discover about two days' worth of new things I'd like to do. You'd be amazed at what I left *out* of the book! But it will be a little relief, I'll bet, when you're home again in a less frenetic, slower-paced world than that of New York. (I don't know where you're from, but I *do* know that wherever it is, it's less frenetic and slower-paced than New York.) Things will be quieter, softer, cooler and you'll heave a sigh of relief. And suddenly you'll miss it. Soon one of the kids will say

"When can we go back?" Then you'll find yourself looking for places you recognize on TV shows and movies set in the city. Finally you realize: You're hooked. There's too much left undone. You've got to go back. With luck, that will be just as the *next* edition of this book comes off the press.

21. Budget Worksheets

This chapter will provide several easy-to-use forms that you can use to plan your big trip. First are two forms for you to gather information about hotels and apartments, and to compare them easily. They're best for talking on the phone with the manager, but if you need to, you can use them by mail or fax, especially if you're coming from outside North America. All the tips and techniques from Chapter 2 are included on the forms.

Next, for readers who will be flying to New York City, is a form you can fill out before you begin speaking to airlines and travel agents. This form, based on the advice in Chapter 3, can help you get the best airfare by outlining your travel requirements so you or your agent can be as flexible as possible.

Finally, the chapter contains a simple budget-planning form you can use to project your expenses, drawing from the suggestions you'll find throughout the book. This budget (like the usual Lain travel budgets) will probably estimate on the high side. It's always been our preference to have money left over rather than to run out before the end. We're pretty conservative financially.

Accommodations Forms

Apartments are ideal if you're staying in New York for a week or more; they're far more home-like than any hotel room. Apartments are normally more economical than hotels and, because they're roomier, are much more comfortable. You can also save money by cooking some of your own meals instead of having to eat every meal at a restaurant. But if you opt for a large hotel room or suite, you can still save money by getting one with a kitchenette. Always talk or write directly to the manager to get the best information and the best price.

Once you've compiled a list of several possible apartments or hotels from the NYCVB booklet *Official NYC Guide*, or from some of the websites listed in the Appendix, you're ready to begin making contact. Telephoning is the best way to gather basic information, with a follow-up letter or fax to the manager of the place you select.

Form 1a—Finding an apartment

1. Hello. I am looking for an apartment in New York City for ___ people. We will arrive on this date, _____ and will leave on _____, a total of ___ nights. There will be ___adults and children whose ages are _____.

2. We would like a…
   ❏ studio apartment
   ❏ 1-bedroom apartment
   ❏ 2-bedroom apartment

Please describe the apartment, the building, and the neighborhood:

3. What is the address of the apartment? What is the nearest subway station?

4. How large is the apartment? What floor is it on? How many beds?

5. What kind of bath/toilet facilities are in the apartment?

6. Does the apartment face the street? How quiet is it? Describe the building and apartment security features.

7. Describe the furnishings and appliances in the apartment. Is there a telephone? A television?

8. Describe the cooking facilities in the apartment. How much storage space is there?

9. Does the apartment have laundry facilities? Air-conditioning?

10. Describe the building. When was it last remodeled? Is there an elevator?

11. How often is the apartment cleaned and linens changed?

12. Describe the neighborhood. Is it residential, commercial, industrial?

13. How far away is the nearest self-service laundry? Grocery store? Bakery?

14. How do we pick up the keys?

15. What is the best price you can give me, including all taxes?

16. Is there any way to reduce it further? (like length of stay, weekend specials, bringing our own linens for extra cots, sleeping bags so we won't require an extra bed, cleaning the apartment ourselves and laundering the sheets and towels, etc.)

17. Are there other dates in about the same time period when the rate would be lower?

18. What credit cards do you accept? How much deposit do you require and when is the balance due?

Thank you. If we decide to rent this apartment, I will confirm this with you within two weeks.

Form 1b—Finding a hotel

1. Hello. I am looking for a hotel in New York City for ___ people. We will arrive on this date, _____ and will leave on _____, a total of ___ nights. There will be ___adults and children whose ages are _____.

2. Where is the hotel? What's the nearest subway station?
3. Do you have a room or suite with cooking facilities? A refrigerator?
4. How large is the room?
5. How is the room furnished?
6. What kind of bath/toilet facilities are in the room?
7. What is the charge for extra people?
8. Are rollaway beds available for extra people?
9. If we don't use a rollaway or bring our own linens for it, is there a deduction? How much?
10. Does the room face the street? How quiet is it? Is there an elevator?
11. Does the room have an alarm clock? Coffee maker? Hair dryer? Refrigerator?
12. Is breakfast provided? What does it consist of?
13. How far away is the nearest self-service laundry? Grocery store? Bakery?
14. What is the best price you can give me, including all taxes?
15. Is there any way to reduce it further? (like length of stay, weekend specials, bringing our own linens for extra cots, sleeping bags so we won't require an extra bed, cleaning the apartment ourselves and laundering the sheets and towels, etc.)
16. Are there other dates in about the same time period when the rate would be lower?
17. What credit cards do you accept? Do you require a deposit?

Thank you. If we decide to rent this room, I will confirm this with you within two weeks.

Once you've gathered information about three or four apartments or hotels, you ought to be able to make a wise and informed choice about where to stay. Contact the manager again and make the booking, and follow up in writing with a letter or fax.

Finding the Best Airfare

Answer these questions for your travel agent or before you sit down to check websites and airlines. They'll help you get the best deal.

Form 2—Air travel requirements

1. How many people traveling? _____
   _____Adults   _____Children under 18 (ages:_____)
                    _____How many students?
   Depending on the route and the time of year, discounts may be available to students or children under certain a age

2. Departure date: _____
   Is this date ❑Fixed or is it ❑Flexible?
   If you can travel during Low Season, airfares may be half or less of High Season (summer months) fares. Avoid Friday, Saturday, Sunday departures.

3. Length of stay? _____days/weeks
   Stays of 7 to 30 days usually qualify for the cheapest rates because business travelers usually stay for less than a week. Avoid return flights on Friday, Saturday, Sunday for better rates.

4. Preferred airline, if any?_____
   If you or another family member works for an airline, you may be eligible for deep discounts. Do you have a frequent flier account with an airline? Do you have enough miles in an account to get one or more tickets free?
5. Preferred airports, if any?_____
   You might save money by driving to a more distant airport where cheaper fares are offered. Price flights from all nearby airports. And remember that prices to all NYC airports are not necessarily the same.

6. Non-stop flight required or connection okay?
   ❑Non-stop only; ❑connection okay
   Unless you live near a city with non-stop service, this isn't an issue: you'll have to connect. But if there's a choice, the connection might be cheaper.

7. Check consolidators.

Some companies buy blocks of tickets from airlines and resell them at a discount. These can be great value, but check companies carefully: some very low advertised prices are scams. Travel agents may know who are the most reputable consolidators.

Armed with this information and these tips, you should be able to find the best fares available. Don't stop watching for sales after you buy your tickets, either. Airlines will often reissue more expensive tickets at sale prices for a service charge.

Your Vacation Budget

Now we get to it: What is it going to take to give your family the vacation of a lifetime? The form is set up to estimate on the high side, but it's a wonderful feeling to come home from a great trip with money left over.

Form 3—Your travel budget

_____1. Travel expenses

Airfare, train tickets, or driving expenses, including meals during layovers or on the train or road, and overnight accommodation if you're driving a long distance.

_____2. Accommodations

from Form 1a or 1b. If you're driving, include the cost of parking your car in this category.

_____3. Food: meals and snacks

• *If you're staying in a hotel, you'll probably eat two or three meals per day in restaurants. If that's the case, allow $25 to $40 per person, per day for meals, depending on the ages of your children.*

• *If you're renting an apartment and plan to fix breakfast and supper at home most of the time, eating only lunch out, figure $10 to $25 per person, per day, a figure which also takes the purchase of groceries into account. It's possible to spend much more, of course, but these figures will provide for you comfortably.*

New York City for Families

Per person/per day ____x number of days ____x number in family
=$_____

_____4. Attractions and sightseeing
There are many free attractions, and the kids get in free to many places that cost their parents. You'll probably spend less than this but let's figure an average of $8 per person per day.
$8 x ____people x ____days =$_____

_____5. Shopping and souvenirs
This is a very personal category. We suggest you give each child a fixed amount, perhaps $20 to $50, or a sum of perhaps $5 to $10 per day to pay for souvenirs, snacks, etc. They can, of course, supplement that with their own money if they wish. Mom and Dad can set their own budget in this category. However, it is best to set a fixed amount in advance. Give the money to your children when you arrive, sor perhaps a little at a time for younger ones.

_____6. Local Transportation
• *The subway: If you buy the unlimited ride MetroCard, the cost is $17 per week. If that's more than you need, you can buy cards for a specific number of rides at $1.50 per ride. But you can easily average 4 rides per day per person, which comes to $42 per week each!*
$17 x ____ people x ____ weeks = $_____

• *Airport Transportation: If you fly into New York and take a taxi to your accommodations, it will cost you at least $30. Public transportation is less convenient but much cheaper. Remember that you have to budget for the return trip, too.*
$3 x ____people = $_____ or <u>$60 to $100</u>

• *Taxi: You might take a taxi occasionally during your visit. Let's budget <u>$30</u>.*

Total Expenses in Categories 1 through 6 above $_____

That's all there is to it. The Lains usually take that bottom line and add another 10 percent, because we'd rather plan for too many expenses than be surprised by extra ones. Put it all together and you've got a pretty good handle on just what this great adventure will cost.

Once you get to New York City and settle into your temporary home, you'll be surprised by how much easier it seemed than it did when you started the planning. Have a great family trip!

Appendix: Websites for Planning Your Trip

Listed below are helpful links and official websites of attractions, as well as selected unofficial websites I think are especially useful. If you find a broken link, or a web address that's changed, please let me know so it can be updated. A page of clickable hotlinks will be posted at the author's *New York City for Families* update page, accessible through *www.interlinkbooks.com/nycforfamilies.html*

Getting There

Amtrak
fares, schedules, and other information about the national passenger rail service
www.amtrak.com

Cheaptickets
discount airfare
cheaptickets.com

Driving in NYC
information about routes, parking regulations, traffic conditions, and more
www.ny.com/transportation/automobiles

Internet Travel Network
travel information from American Express
www.itn.com

Lowestfare
discount airfare
lowestfare.com

Microsoft Expedia
popular general travel site
www.expedia.com

Priceline
name your own price for airfare and hotels, but watch restrictions
www.priceline.com

Travelocity
good general travel site
www.travelocity.com

Accommodations—Apartment Services

Aaah! Bed & Breakfast
nybnb.com

As You Like It Bed & Breakfast
newyork.citysearch.com/profile/7080540

Gamut Realty
www.gamutnyc.com

Habitat New York
nyhabitat-vacation.com

Maison International
maisonintl.com/index.htm

Manhattan Getaways
www.manhattangetaways.com

Manhattan Lodgings
manhattanlodgings.com

Oxbridge Apartments
www.oxbridgeny.com

Accommodations—Hotels and Suites with Kitchenettes

Allerton Hotel
very basic, but inexpensive
www.allerton-hotel.com

Hotel San Carlos
www.sancarloshotel.com

Manhattan East Suite Hotels
mostly expensive, but a few bargains
mesuite.com

Off Soho Suites
offsoho.com

Radio City Apartments
radiocityapartments.com

Accommodations—Hotel Listings

CentralParking.com Hotel Listings
www.centralparkingny.com/accomodations.html

Carter Hotel
no cooking facilities, but perhaps the most inexpensive Midtown hotel
carterhotel.com

New York Citysearch
newyork.citysearch.com/section/hotels_visitors

New York Convention & Visitors Bureau Hotel Listings
www.nycvisit.com/site_hotels.html

NY.com
www.ny.com/hotels/all.hotels.html

SearchNYC
good list of budget hotels
www.searchnyc.com/hotels.html

TravelWeb
many independent hotels available
travelweb.com

Media

New York *Daily News*
populist tabloid
www.nydailynews.com

***New York* Magazine**
nymag.com

New York *Post*
sensationalistic tabloid
www.nypostonline.com

New York *Times*
probably America's best daily; requires free registration
www.nytimes.com

NYC Radio Stations
guide to AM and FM stations
www.nyradioguide.com

NYC Television Stations
unofficial list of stations and links
tvschedules.about.com/tvradio/tvschedules/library/cities/blnyc.htm

***Time Out* Magazine, New York edition**
www.timeout.com/newyork/index.html

Arrival

Immigration and Naturalization Service
U.S. government site with free downloadable forms, but hard
to navigate.
www.ins.gov

Immigration Services
visa requirements; also offers immigration forms for a fee.
www.visa-forms.com

LaGuardia Airport Information
www.panynj.gov/aviation/lgahomemain.htm

Kennedy Airport Information
www.panynj.gov/aviation/jfkhomemain.htm

Newark Airport Information
www.panynj.gov/aviation/ewrhomemain.htm

Getting Around

Circle Line Cruises
spectacular views from the rivers and New York Harbor
www.circleline.com

Metropolitan Transit Authority
subways, buses, commuter rail—one-stop shopping
www.mta.nyc.ny.us

NY Waterway
harbor cruises and ferries to Yankee Stadium and Shea Stadium
www.nywaterway.com

Roosevelt Island Tram
www.rioc.com/transportation.html

Staten Island Ferry
www.ci.nyc.ny.us/html/dot/html/get_around/ferry/statfery.html

Attractions

American Museum of the Moving Image
www.ammi.org

American Museum of Natural History
amnh.org

Americas Society
www.americas-society.org

Asia Society
www.asiasociety.org

Bloomingdale's
www.bloomingdales.com

Brooklyn Academy of Music
www.bam.org

Brooklyn Botanic Gardens
www.bbg.org

Brooklyn Bridge (unofficial site)
www.endex.com/gf/buildings/bbridge/bbridge.html

Brooklyn Museum of Art
www.brooklynart.org

Bronx Zoo (International Wildlife Conservation Center)
www.wcs.org/home/zoos/bronxzoo

Brooklyn Children's Museum
www.bchildmus.org

Carnegie Hall
www.carnegiehall.org

Cathedral of St. John the Divine
www.stjohndivine.org

Chelsea Piers
www.chelseapiers.com

Children's Museum of Manhattan
www.cmom.org

Chinatown
www.chinatown-online.com/nychinatown.htm

Coney Island
www.astroland.com
www.wonderwheel.com

Empire State Building
www.esbnyc.com

Ellis Island
www.ellisisland.org

Federal Hall
www.nps.gov/feha

Frick Collection
www.frick.org

Fraunces Tavern
www.fieldtrip.com/ny/24251778.htm

Grand Central Terminal
www.grandcentralterminal.com

Guggenheim Museum
www.guggenheim.org

Historic Richmond Town
www.preserve.org/hht/richmond/town

Intrepid Sea Air Space Museum
www.intrepidmuseum.org

Japan Society
www.japansociety.org

Jewish Museum
www.thejewishmuseum.org

Lazer Park
www.lazerpark.com

Lincoln Center
www.lincolncenter.org

Lower East Side Tenement Museum
www.tenement.org

Macy's Department Store
www.macys.com

Madison Square Garden
www.thegarden.com

Manhattan Mall
www.manhattanmallny.com

Metropolitan Museum of Art
www.metmuseum.org

Museo del Barrio
www.elmuseo.org

Museum for African Art
www.africanart.com

Museum of American Folk Art
www.folkartmuseum.net

Museum of the City of New York
www.mcny.org

Museum of Jewish Heritage
www.mjhnyc.org

Museum of Modern Art
www.moma.org

Museum of Television and Radio
www.mtr.org

National Museum of the American Indian
www.nmai.si.edu

New York Aquarium
www.nyaquarium.com

New York Botanical Gardens
www.nybg.org

NYC Fire Museum
www.nyfd.com/museum

New York City Police Museum
www.nycpolicemuseum.org

New York Hall of Science
www.nyhallsci.org

New York Historical Society
www.nyhistory.org

New York Public Library
www.nypl.org

New York Transit Museum
www.mta.nyc.ny.us/museum

Old Merchant's House
www.fieldtrip.com/ny/27771089.htm

Prospect Park
www.prospectpark.org

P.S. 1
www.ps1.org

Queens Museum of Art
www.queensmuse.org

Radio City Music Hall
www.radiocity.com

Riverside Church
www.theriversidechurchny.org

St. Patrick's Cathedral
www.ny-archdiocese.org/pastoral/cathedral_about.html

Snug Harbor Cultural Center
www.snug-harbor.org

Sony Wonder Technology Lab
wondertechlab.sony.com

South Street Seaport
www.southstseaport.org
www.southstreetseaport.com

Statue of Liberty
www.nps.gov/stli/

Temple Emanu-el
www.emanuelnyc.org/home.html

Theodore Roosevelt Birthplace
www.nps.gov/thrb

Times Square Visitors Center
www.timessquarebid.org/visitor/Visitors_Center/visitors_center.html

Trinity Church
www.trinitywallstreet.org

United Nations
www.un.org

Whitney Museum of American Art
www.whitney.org

World Trade Center Observatory
www.wtc-top.com

Zoos
This is the site for the Bronx Zoo, with links to other NYC zoos
www.wcs.org/home/zoos/bronxzoo

Theater

Comprehensive site with information about shows, prices, ticket buying, and shows for kids
www.nytheatre.com

Official site for ordering tickets for Broadway shows
www.ticketmaster.com

For the latest updates to *New York City for Families*,
check out our page on the web at:

www.interlinkbooks.com/nycforfamilies.html

Of related interest

Paris for Families
by Larry Lain

From the top of the Eiffel Tower to the creepy Catacombes below the city, the author of the highly acclaimed _London for Families_ now delivers a comprehensive survey of Paris's main attractions, designed especially to help families plan a vacation that is fun and affordable.

Paris for Families is your guide for the most memorable family holiday of your life, everything you need to know about making the most of your money, finding a home away from home in the city, and putting together an itinerary that is both practical and fun.

288 pages • b&w illus. & photos • ISBN 1-56656-360-7 • $15.00 pb

London for Families
by Larry Lain and Michael Lain

"An eminently useful guide for planning a first or even a second trip to London... of help not only to families but to first time visitors to London of any age, including college students and seniors. Recommended."

—Library Journal

"...an accessible, well-organized and even friendly guide to a fun and hassle free trip abroad. London for Families is a must-have."
—Independent Publisher

288 pages • b&w illus. & maps • ISBN 1-56656-337-2 • $14.95 pb

A Traveller's History of the U.S.A.
by Dan McInerney

A Traveller's History of the U.S.A. guides today's travellers through a general history of the people and places of America. Starting with the lay of the land and the cultures of its first inhabitants, it examines the rise of European colonies, the emergence of a new nation, and the tragic, triumphant, twisting course of its republican experiment, right up to the present day.

480 pages • maps & line drawings • ISBN 1-56656-283-X • $15.95 pb

Interlink Bestselling Travel Publications

The Traveller's History Series

The Traveller's History series is designed for travellers who want more historical background on the country they are visiting than can be found in a tour guide. Each volume offers a complete and authoritative history of the country from the earliest times up to the present day. A Gazetteer cross-referenced to the main text pinpoints the historical importance of sights and towns. Illustrated with maps and line drawings, this literate and lively series makes ideal before-you-go reading, and is just as handy tucked into suitcase or backpack.

A Traveller's History of Australia	$14.95 pb
A Traveller's History of the Caribbean	$14.95 pb
A Traveller's History of China	$14.95 pb
A Traveller's History of England	$14.95 pb
A Traveller's History of France	$14.95 pb
A Traveller's History of Greece	$14.95 pb
A Traveller's History of India	$14.95 pb
A Traveller's History of Ireland	$14.95 pb
A Traveller's History of Italy	$14.95 pb
A Traveller's History of Japan	$14.95 pb
A Traveller's History of London	$14.95 pb
A Traveller's History of Mexico	$14.95 pb
A Traveller's History of North Africa	$15.95 pb
A Traveller's History of Paris	$14.95 pb
A Traveller's History of Russia	$14.95 pb
A Traveller's History of Scotland	$14.95 pb
A Traveller's History of Spain	$14.95 pb
A Traveller's History of Turkey	$14.95 pb
A Traveller's History of the U.S.A.	$15.95 pb

The Traveller's Wine Guides

Illustrated with specially commissioned photographs (wine usually seems to be made in attractive surroundings) as well as maps, the books in this series describe the wine-producing regions of each country, recommend itineraries, list wineries, describe the local cuisines, suggest wine bars and restaurants, and provide a mass of practical information–much of which is not readily available elsewhere.

A Traveller's Wine Guide to France	$19.95 pb
A Traveller's Wine Guide to Germany	$17.95 pb
A Traveller's Wine Guide to Italy	$19.95 pb
A Traveller's Wine Guide to Spain	$17.95 pb

The Independent Walker Series

This unique series is designed for visitors who enjoy walking and getting off the beaten track. In addition to their value as general guides, each volume is peerless as a walker's guide, allowing travellers to see all of the great sites, enjoy the incomparable beauty of the countryside, and maintain a high level of physical fitness while travelling through the popular tourist destinations. Each guide includes:

• Practical information on thirty-five extraordinary short walks (all planned as day hikes and are between 2 and 9 miles), including: how to get there, where to stay, trail distance, walking time, difficulty rating, explicit trail directions and a vivid general description of the trail and local sights.

• Numerous itineraries: The Grand Tour which embraces all thirty-five walks; regional itineraries; and thematic itineraries.

• One planning map for the itineraries and thirty-five detailed trail maps.

• Trail notes broken down into an easy-to-follow checklist format.

• A "Walks-at-a-Glance" section which provides capsule summariesof all the walks.

• Black and white photographs.

• Before-you-go helpful hints.

The Independent Walker's Guide to France	$14.95 pb
The Independent Walker's Guide to Great Britain	$14.95 pb
The Independent Walker's Guide to Italy	$14.95 pb
The Independent Walker's Guide to Ireland	$14.95 pb

Wild Guides

An unrivalled series of illustrated guidebooks to the wild places far from home and work: the long walks, mountain hideaways, woods, moors, sea coasts and remote islands where travellers can still find a refuge from the modern world.

"The Wild Guides will be enjoyed by everyone who hopes to find unspoiled places."
—The Times (London)

Wild Britain	$19.95 pb
Wild France	$19.95 pb
Wild Ireland	$19.95 pb
Wild Italy	$19.95 pb
Wild Spain	$19.95 pb

Cities of the Imagination

A new and innovative series offering in-depth cultural, historical and literary guides to the great cities of the world. More than ordinary guidebooks, they introduce the visitor or armchair traveller to each city's unique present-day identity and its links with the past.

Buenos Aires: A Cultural and Literary Companion	$15.00 pb
Edinburgh: A Cultural and Literary Companion	$15.00 pb
Havana: A Cultural and Literary Companion	$15.00 pb
Kingston: A Cultural and Literary Companion	$15.00 pb

Lisbon: A Cultural and Literary Companion	$15.00 pb
Madrid: A Cultural and Literary Companion	$15.00 pb
Mexico City: A Cultural and Literary Companion	$15.00 pb
Oxford: A Cultural and Literary Companion	$15.00 pb
Rome: A Cultural and Literary Companion	$15.00 pb
Venice: A Cultural and Literary Companion	$15.00 pb

The Spectrum Guides

Each title in the series includes over 200 full-color photographs and provides a comprehensive and detailed description of the country together with all the essential data that tourists, business visitors or students are likely to require.

Spectrum Guide to Ethiopia	$22.95 pb
Spectrum Guide to India	$22.95 pb
Spectrum Guide to Jordan	$22.95 pb
Spectrum Guide to Malawi	$23.95 pb
Spectrum Guide to Maldives	$22.95 pb
Spectrum Guide to Mauritius	$19.95 pb
Spectrum Guide to Nepal	$22.95 pb
Spectrum Guide to Pakistan	$22.95 pb
Spectrum Guide to Tanzania	$22.95 pb
Spectrum Guide to Uganda	$19.95 pb
Spectrum Guide to the United Arab Emirates	$23.95 pb
Spectrum Guide to the Zimbabwe	$23.95 pb

The In Focus Guides

This new series of country guides is designed for travellers and students who want to understand the wider picture and build up an overall knowledge of a country. Each In Focus guide is a lively and thought-provoking introduction to the country's people, politics and culture.

Belize in Focus	$12.95 pb
Bolivia in Focus	$12.95 pb
Brazil in Focus	$12.95 pb
Chile in Focus	$12.95 pb
Costa Rica in Focus	$12.95 pb
Cuba in Focus	$12.95 pb
The Dominican Republic in Focus	$12.95 pb
Eastern Caribbean in Focus	$12.95 pb
Ecuador in Focus	$12.95 pb
Guatemala in Focus	$12.95 pb
Haiti in Focus	$12.95 pb
Jamaica in Focus	$12.95 pb
Mexico in Focus	$12.95 pb
Nicaragua in Focus	$12.95 pb
Peru in Focus	$12.95 pb

We encourage you to support your local independent bookseller